INSIGHT ○ GUIDES

EXPLORE

BEIJING

D1372605

⊙ Walking Eye App

Your Insight Guide purchase includes a free download of the destination's corresponding eBook. It is available now from the free Walking Eye container app in the App Store and Google Play. Simply download the Walking Eye container app to access the eBook dedicated to your purchased book. The app also features free information on local events taking place and activities you can enjoy during your stay, with the option to book them. In addition, premium content for a wide range of other destinations is available to purchase in-app.

HOW TO DOWNLOAD THE WALKING EYE APP

Available on purchase of this guide only.

1. Visit our website: www.insightguides.com/walkingeye
2. Download the Walking Eye container app to your smartphone (this will give you access to your free eBook and the ability to purchase other products)
3. Select the scanning module in the Walking Eye container app
4. Scan the QR Code on this page – you will be asked to enter a verification word from the book as proof of purchase
5. Download your free eBook* for travel information on the go

* Other destination apps and eBooks are available for purchase separately or are free with the purchase of the Insight Guide book

CONTENTS

Introduction

Directory

Credits

Best Routes

FOOD AND DRINK

Beijing is home to some excellent cuisines, both foreign and local. Sample fine dining at Temple Restaurant Beijing, eat like an emperor (route 4) or sample classic Beijing snacks (route 6).

RECOMMENDED ROUTES FOR...

GOOD WEATHER

A really beautiful day is a rare thing in Beijing, so make the most of it. Climb the Fragrant Hills (route 13) or wander by the idyllic lakes that dot Beijing's centre (route 4).

MODERN CULTURE

Immerse yourself in modern art at the 798 Art District (route 12), or go for smaller, more select galleries near the Forbidden City (route 6) or the museum at the Poly Plaza (route 10).

OUTDOOR ENTHUSIASTS

See the Great Wall of China outside of Beijing (route 14). Explore the hills closer to the city (route 13) or climb up another for great vantage on an ancient Ming-era town (route 15).

RELIGIOUS CENTRES

Buddhism is China's most deep-rooted religion and the Lama Temple is the best spot to soak in that atmosphere (route 3). Beijing is also home to a very old mosque (route 7) and lovely Catholic cathedrals (route 2).

SHOPPING

Get your fill of modern articles at the Silk Market (route 10), or head to Dazhalan and Liulichang (route 7) for products you'll find only in Beijing.

THE GRAND TOUR

Start from Tiananmen Square and proceed through the Forbidden City (route 1). Hit the Temple of Heaven (route 5) and then the Ming Tombs to see a fitting end for a Son of Heaven (route 14).

BEIJING PAST AND PRESENT

Stroll through the Foreign Legation Quarter (route 2) and walk through Dongsi to see ancient hutong neighbourhoods (route 10). Then contrast old Beijing with the new CBD (route 10) and the space-age Olympic facilities (route 11).

INTRODUCTION

An introduction to Beijing's geography, customs and culture, plus illuminating background information on cuisine, history and what to do when you're there.

Zhengyangmen

EXPLORE BEIJING

Apart from its immediately apparent structures of unparalleled grandiosity, Beijing's greatest treasures are hidden, tucked into hutongs (alleyways) and corners, best accessible through patient, on-the-ground exploration.

The Beijing municipality covers 16,808 sq km (6,488 sq miles). To its south is the fertile North China Plain and to the east, the Bohai Sea. To the west, north-west and north-east are mountain ranges. Its location as the imperial seat of several dynasties, including the Liao, Jin, Yuan, Ming and Qing, was selected both for reasons of *feng shui* – mountains to the north and water or plains to the south are considered auspicious – and of defence – a series of mountain passes shield Beijing from the northern nomadic tribes.

CITY LAYOUT

At the heart of Beijing is the Forbidden City, which used to be the imperial palace and is now a gigantic open-air museum. To its south is the world's largest public square, Tiananmen Square, where Communist buildings and monuments hold court. Immediately south of the square is an area of rapidly gentrifying *hutongs* (alleyways), a tourist-friendly taste of old Beijing and its traditional businesses, reimagined for modern convenience.

To the Forbidden City's east is Wangfujing, Beijing's premier shopping street. Further east is Chaoyang district, where international businesses, skyscrapers and expatriates gather. To the west and the north of the Forbidden City are the pretty back lakes, home to atmospheric *hutongs*, bars and cafés.

The ancient plans of the imperial city still dictate the shape and flow of the modern capital, though not always in a positive way. The city wall of the Ming and Qing dynasties, demolished in the 1950s, defines Erhuan Lu (Second Ring Road), the primary artery of the city. The modernisation efforts of the past decades – arterials, Soviet-inspired ring roads, skyscrapers and overpasses – have not changed the city's essential layout.

Urban sprawl

Beijing's roads (not to mention its air), designed long before the automobile, simply cannot handle the burden of a population enamoured with cars, especially when more than a thousand new vehicles are added to the roads each day. To make matters worse, the traditional city was made up of one- or

two-storey buildings, none taller than the Forbidden City. This means the population density in the old city within the Second Ring Road is very low. Beijing has thus expanded outward into suburban sprawl, with endless forests of identical apartment buildings.

Traditional Beijing

Since the Yuan dynasty, established by the Mongolians, Beijingers have lived in single-storey homes with tile roofs, which face a central courtyard and are protected by high walls. These are set within a *maze* of hutong, some dating back many centuries and one of Beijing's most alluring sights.

One *hutong* area not to be missed is that around the Bell and Drum towers and the back lakes of the Forbidden City. Strolling or cycling around the area is a delightful experience. There are tiny workshops dimly lit by a single bulb, elderly men carrying their songbirds in cages, street vendors selling steaming buns – see these before they disappear.

NAVIGATING THE CITY

Moving through the city is relatively convenient apart from during morning and evening rush hours that can last several hours. Unfortunately, these affect both taxi and subway journeys though the extensive underground rail network and armies of patrolling taxis are still far and away the easiest ways to get around.

Though Beijing is ostensibly laid out on a grid, navigation is still tricky. The names of streets often change halfway, or differ from one another only by a single syllable. Sometimes they are marked with one name on the map, and referred to by another in speech.

North, south, inside, outside

North and south, inside and outside – these were crucial concepts to the planners of the old city. The Forbidden City had to have its back to the north and face south, laid out on a north–south axis. It may be worth learning the Chinese words for north, south, east and west (*bei, nan, dong* and *xi*, respectively), as many streets have mirror-image counterparts elsewhere, the result of a traditional love of symmetry. The concepts of *nei* and *wai* (inside and outside, respectively) once took the emperor's throne as the centre – now these terms most often refer to the inside or outside of Erhuan Lu, the Second Ring Road. Thus, Chaoyangmen Neidajie is the large street (*dajie*) that runs inside (*nei*) the Second Ring Road from Chaoyangmen Bridge, and Chaoyangmen Beixiaojie is the small street (*xiaojie*) that runs north (*bei*) from Chaoyangmen Neidajie.

Street numbers exist, but they are essentially useless for navigation. Taxi drivers will know the names of major streets, as well as the locations of overpasses, hotels, shopping malls and other landmarks.

Once on foot, you will find things are not necessarily easier. Pavements peter out unexpectedly, turn into car parks or shopfronts, or there are trees planted smack in their middle. Overpasses are sporadic. Many drivers completely disregard the rights of pedestrians, turning without warning or roaring through crosswalks with horns blaring. Walking in Beijing takes some getting used to – the best tactic is to stick to the centre of pedestrian herds.

An Olympian legacy

Perhaps the greatest physical legacy of Beijing's hosting of the 2008 Olympic Games was the public transit upgrades. Three subway lines had opened in time for the games and as of 2015, Beijingers have access to 18 lines, which altogether comprise one of the world's largest metro systems – the second longest in the world, after the Shanghai Metro. It is the world's busiest in terms of the number of annual riders, so further expansion to fully meet the city's needs is planned. Beijing Airport transitted over 86 million passengers in 2014, while the rail network's Beijing South station boasts some of the world's fastest conventional trains, rushing towards Tianjin at a top speed of 350kmh (220mph).

BEIJINGERS

Beijing has a population of around 22 million, making it China's second-largest city after Shanghai. Han Chinese make up about 96 percent of the population. Around seven million migrant workers from other parts of the country and more than 100,000 foreigners live in Beijing.

Beijing residents have a unique reputation among Chinese from other parts of the country. As the seat of imperial power for a thousand years, Beijing cannot help but boast a certain historical status. True Beijing residents can often find royal blood in their family trees, or at least an association with the Banner Houses of the Qing dynasty. At the same time, Beijing's weighty political atmosphere has slowed its development in many ways. Compared with cities like Guangzhou or Shanghai, parts of the capital can appear behind the times, even frumpy – Shanghainese take a particular pleasure in calling Beijingers 'peasants'. The typical, traditional Beijing resident is gruff, plain-spoken and brooks no nonsense.

The new generation of millennial urbanites, however, consider themselves to be living in a fully international city and take for granted everything that entails. They converse with friends via Weibo (the Chinese equivalent of Twitter) and other online platforms (homegrown ones have more traction due to the 'great firewall' blocking the likes of Facebook and Youtube) or over coffee at Starbucks, aspire to speak several languages, and seek individuality in

The Great Wall

DON'T LEAVE BEIJING WITHOUT...

Exploring the hutongs on two wheels. This is the best way to get a feel for the old city. Bicycles can be hired from a point just east of the Drum Tower or at various spots around Houhai for about 10 yuan per hour, plus a deposit. For the more serious rider, Natooke (19 Wudaoying Hutong; tel: 8402 6925; daily 10.30am–7pm) hires vintage Flying Pigeon and fixed gear bikes by the day.

Checking out Beijing's burgeoning art scene. After you've finished touring the iconic 798 factory district, swing by Red Gate in Chongwenmen for cutting-edge contemporary Chinese artists in a restored guard tower, the Poly Museum for beautiful cultural artefacts or one of the numerous small hutong galleries to see what the local creative types are up to.

Taking an early-morning walk in the park. Chinese get up early year round to practice Tai Chi, calligraphy, music and dancing in these public spaces, which open up a window onto local culture. Best bets are Coal Hill Park, Ditan Park and the park surrounding the Temple of Heaven.

Partying like the locals do, with karaoke! Chinese style ballading, known as KTV, involves renting a private room, decked out with couches, a TV screen and a sound system, and belting out the hits with your friends for a few hours. A typical parlour is huge, decked out in cheesy kitsch, and a few higher-end places even have goofy but fun themed rooms.

Catching a gig at one of the city's music venues. Beijing's music calendar could be the best in China, ranging from Mongolian folk to heavy metal to indie rock with Chinese characteristics. See the local English language listings magazines for the latest bands.

Sampling regional Chinese cuisine. As the capital, Beijing offers everything from spicy Sichuanese, hearty Xinjiang and fragrant Yunnanese, all as authentic as they come. A great place to start is at the provincial Chinese restaurants, located in what are essentially embassies for their home province, scattered around the city.

Getting a taste of tea culture at Maliandao, Beijing's tea market. Casually browse the over 1,000 tea retailers, restaurants and importers offering top blends, with many offering free samples of everything from everyday blends to boutique leaves.

Visiting the Summer Palace by boat. Travel in the style Cixi would have been accustomed to. Craft leave from Purple Bamboo Park every hour in summer with the voyage to the palace's south gate taking about an hour. Call 6852-9428 for more information.

Taking a cultural class. Deepen your understanding with an educational class. The Hutong (tel: 6404 3355, www.thehutong.com) offers relaxed group cooking classes on regional cuisines, covering necessary skills from noodle pulling to knife handling, followed by a meal of your creations.

A streetside pitstop for tea and snacks

their choice of clothing, musical taste and religion. Unsurprisingly, there is a yawning generation gap between these modern youngsters and parents whose jobs, housing and furniture may have been assigned to them by a work unit and who expect to have a say in almost every aspect of their children's lives.

It used to be that you could not tell rich Beijingers from poor, and lavishness was reserved for interiors only. This attitude is still reflected in the appearance of the streetsides and older suburbs that often seem unnecessarily run down. But duck behind a wall or go through a doorway, and an entirely new scene reveals itself. As Beijing becomes increasingly conscious of its status as a global capital, however, both the city and its people are beginning to change. An extraordinarily vast amount of money was spent on eye-catching modern architecture and a mass makeover of the city in the run-up to the 2008 Olympic Games, and house-proud residents and businesses beautified their neighbourhoods so as not to look bad by comparison. Yet as the city becomes ever more present on the world stage, an influx of Chinese from the countryside seeking opportunity and widespread property speculation has driven property values to among the world's highest, making home ownership simply not an option for many Chinese.

CITY RHYTHMS

Beijing is awake and bustling by 7am. Even going out as early as 5.30am will reveal aspects of city life others never glimpse upon. If you visit the parks in the early morning or the lakes at twilight, you can get a sense of what city life used to be like. Twenty years ago, lights were out and the city was dead quiet by 8pm, but modern lifestyles are pushing bedtimes later and later, to the extent that some neighbourhoods never sleep at all.

This early-rising tendency, combined with the remnants of an extraordinarily inefficient bureaucratic system, means that it is best to get official business done in the morning. Less modernised government offices are reluctant to do much of anything after 3pm. Massive (and seemingly unnecessary) quantities of paperwork are the norm as well, and it is usually a good idea to carry identification and official documents with you at all times.

Still, this is a far cry from the bad old days of the 1970s and 1980s, when shops displayed goods but refused to sell them, restaurant staff served customers if, and only if, they felt like it, and personal connections were needed to obtain a telephone line. The concepts of service and efficiency have gathered great strides in the private sector – and increasingly in the public sector, too.

Bicycles, bicycles everywhere in Beijing

TOP TIPS FOR VISITING BEIJING

When to go. Beijing winters are cold, dry and windy; summers are unrelentingly hot and muggy. It is best to go either in April/May or late September/October, when the skies are clear (apart from the spring sandstorms that blow in from the Gobi Desert) and strolling is a real pleasure.

Observing the smoking ban. If you're a smoker, cigarettes are cheap, potent and plentiful. But you can't light up just anywhere: since 2015, Beijing has enacted a smoking ban in all public places including bars, restaurants and offices, and it is increasingly enforced in urban areas. You might not have to pay the fine, but you might be asked to finish it outside.

Haggling. Be stubborn when bargaining, trying not to appear too keen. Make your first offer no more than 50 percent of the shopkeeper's initial asking price. Be persistent, keep smiling and walk away if you find the price unacceptable.

Go prepared. Almost no public WCs have toilet paper. Buy an inexpensive pack of tissue from a corner store and carry it with you always.

Be the first there. Get the most out of Beijing's scenic spots by arriving as early as you can: at major sites like the Forbidden City, you'll be jostling with thousands of other of Chinese tourists brought in by the busload.

Navigate the 'great firewall'. Sign up for a Virtual Private Network (VPN) service before you leave. This will allow you to bypass the strict government control over the internet, and give you an opportunity to show off you best travel snaps to those back home on social media.

Smile please! If you're Western, don't be surprised if a complete stranger asks to take a photograph with you – you might be the first foreigner they have ever seen! If you're keen, smile and revel in your minute of celebrity.

Cheap calls. Avoid roaming charges by picking up a cheap handset or registering for a local SIM card. A basic number can be picked up easily for less than 100RMB from one of the bountiful number of China Mobile or China Unicom shops on street corners, though you might need to bring a friend who speaks Chinese.

Breathe easy. If Beijing's notoriously bad air is unbearable, do like the Chinese and pick up a pollution mask from a local store. Look for one that says N95 on the package, meaning the filter blocks out 95 per cent of all particulate matter.

Gift ideas. If you're planning to stay a while or will be using a guide for an extended time, consider bringing a gift from your home country. Something simple that can't be found easily within China is best, like branded candy or small cosmetics.

Communication. Try to learn a few words of the local language – you don't have to be fluent, as even a few basic words like 'xie xie' will be well received.

Lamian noodle chef

FOOD AND DRINK

Eating is central to Chinese culture – it is the main activity of most celebratory occasions, key to family time and a necessary element in forging all relationships. Small wonder, then, that one of Beijing's greatest riches is its restaurants.

The range of eating options in this city is enormous, from street vendors roasting sweet potatoes for a few yuan to Western restaurants dishing up meals with the high cost and service charge you'd expect to pay in London or New York. Thankfully for tourists, Beijing also offers cuisines from the country's various regions and from around the world at reasonable prices. In recent years, significantly fancier options have also been added – the worldwide cult of restaurants opened by personality chefs has finally come to the once-staid capital.

BEIJING AND REGIONAL CUISINES

Many dishes classified as Beijing-style actually originated from other parts of the kingdom, then perfected and embellished in the imperial court. Beijing cuisine makes liberal use of strong flavours from ingredients such as garlic, ginger, spring onion and coriander. Beijing's most famous traditional snack stalls live on at Jiumen Xiaochi, a well-known courtyard eatery that stands by Houhai lake. The vendors serve time-honoured culinary creations such as flash-boiled tripe, bean juice, wontons, sticky rice cakes and choice cuts from boiled sheep's head. The dishes of the north tend to be heartier, with noodles and steamed or fried bread, rather than rice, as the staple.

Diverse styles of the fancier 'imperial cuisine' are available in many restaurants around the city. The most common is the Manchu-Han Complete Feast *(manhan quanxi)*, which strives to replicate the dining habits and options of Qing-dynasty royalty, often Empress Dowager Cixi in particular. Other variations include Tan Family cuisine, favoured by a gourmand Qing official, and dishes inspired by those in Cao Xueqin's famous novel, *Dream of the Red Chamber*.

Jianbing, Beijing's most popular street snack, originated in Tianjin. It is a kind of pancake made with egg and spring onion, filled with crunchy, deep-fried dough sticks and garnished with chilli sauce and coriander. The most famous Beijing dish is Peking duck. Another popular meal, especially in winter, is Mongolian hot pot – slivers of mutton plunged into a trough of boiling water, fondue-style.

A creative bean curd dish

Roasting Peking duck

Beijing is also blessed with an excellent representation of food from all over the country. Favourite cuisines include Sichuan, Xinjiang (Uyghur), Yunnanese and Hunanese, and there is no shortage of Shaanxi noodle huts. Those in the know seek out provincial representative offices (*zhujing banshichu*, sort of mini-embassies belonging to each province), each of which has an attached restaurant serving that province's food.

Look around also for some weirder options – Cultural Revolution dining, North Korean food, and even dining in complete darkness in a restaurant with no lights.

PEKING DUCK

The earliest mention of Beijing's most famous dish, Peking duck, can be traced back to a 12th-century cookbook. Numerous restaurants in the city now serve this dish, but the most authentic spot to savour the bird is one of Quanjude's restaurants. The first Quanjude restaurant opened in 1864 in Qianmen (see page 33).

To prepare the ambrosial Peking duck, the bird's unbroken skin is inflated like a balloon, filled with water and glazed with sugar. The duck is then roasted in an oven heated by burning the wood of fruit trees such as date, peach and pear. When the roast duck arrives, you fill your own pancakes at the table. Use your chopsticks to pick up some spring onion and use it as a kind of paint brush to dab a salty *hoisin* bean sauce on the pancake. Add one or two pieces of duck, roll the pancake and enjoy. Part of the art of this cuisine is to make use of the entire duck, and some restaurants claim to make more than 300 different duck dishes, to be sampled while the duck is being roasted. If you are adventurous, try dishes like the cold mustard duck web (from their feet), deep-fried duck liver with sesame and fried duck hearts with chilli sauce.

DRINKS

Those hoping for local booze to match the food may be disappointed. The beer is weak, and China's greatest contribution to the pantheon of alcohols is 'white liquor' *(baijiu)*, best described as two-parts petrol, one-part French perfume. If you can find them, get a bottle of 'yellow liquor' *(huangjiu)* or rice wine *(mijiu)*, both far superior to their clear cousin. *Baijiu* is, unfortunately, a staple at business dinners, where drinking contests can influence the outcome of deals.

> ## Food and drink
>
> Throughout this guide, we have used the following price ranges to denote the approximate cost of a two-course meal for one with an alcoholic drink:
> $$$ = over 200 yuan
> $$ = 100–200 yuan
> $ = 50–100 yuan

Contemporary art knock-offs

SHOPPING

Growing affluence in Beijing means that for many, individualism now comes with a high price tag. New stores open almost every day. This is 'Socialism with Chinese characteristics', as the government calls it, or simply 'unbridled consumerism'.

International brands are aggressively expanding in Beijing, particularly in its gleaming new shopping developments. For local arts and crafts, the smaller streets and markets are still a better choice.

SPECIALITY MARKETS

The **Silk Market** (Xiushui Shichang; daily 9am–6pm) is located in a four-storey building at the Yong'anli subway stop. Its brand-name knock-offs are often targeted for intellectual property violation, but the 20,000 shoppers a day keep the store's doors open. Clothing, accessories, jackets and bags abound. It's a great place to get cheap tailored clothing – just remember to knock more than half off the initial asking price when bargaining.

There are several other good places to buy silk fabrics: **Yuan Long Silk Store** (north gate of the Temple of Heaven; daily 9am–6.30pm) and **Ruifuxiang Silk and Cotton Fabric Store** (Dazhalan Jie; daily 9am–7.30pm).

Hongqiao Market (daily 8.30am–7pm), opposite the east gate of the Temple of Heaven on Tiantan Lu, has antique clocks and Mao statues, as well as freshwater pearls and inexpensive reproduction antiques.

For your computer-related needs, head to Haidian district's Zhongguancun, also known as Beijing's Silicon Valley, or if you're in the eastern part of the city, to Bainaohui on the north side of Chaoyangmenwai Dajie, nearby Dongyue Temple.

ANTIQUES AND HANDICRAFTS

For antiques and traditional handicrafts, try **Liulichang** or the craft stores along **Guozijian Jie** or Nanluoguxiang. Further afield, but considered the most reliable source of collectables and memorabilia of all sorts, is **Panjiayuan Market** (Panjiayuan Jiuhuo Shichang; daily 7am–6.30pm, but it is best to go very early on a weekend morning) located just west of the Panjiayuan Bridge on the Dongsanhuan Donglu (East Third Ring Road). Organised much like a flea market, the outdoor stalls at Panjiayuan cover a large area and sell a large variety of objects, from reproduction ceramics to genuine antiques and curios, as well as

Communist memorabilia for sale

Cultural Revolution-era posters and souvenirs and their reproductions. The weekend welcomes a large junk section with anything from plastic bathtubs to used bicycle bearings. Another place to look for curios is the **Beijing Antique City** (Beijing Guwancheng; daily 9.30am–6pm) at West Huawei Bridge, Dongsanhuan Nanlu (East Third Ring Road).

Note that it is illegal to export antiques that date from prior to 1795. Those that can be taken out of China must carry a small red seal or sticker, or have one affixed by the Cultural Relics Bureau. Beware of fakes: producing new 'antiques' (and the seal) is a thriving industry in China.

SHOPPING AREAS

Three lively shopping streets cater to Beijing's shoppers: **Wangfujing**, **Xidan** and **Dongdan**, all running north from Dongchang'an Jie. They offer inexpensive local goods from age-old Beijing brands, with clothing bargains. The **Beijing Painting & Calligraphy Store** (289 Wangfujing Dajie; daily 8.30am–7pm) has four floors of arts, crafts and jewellery. Further north, on the east side of Wangfujing is the **Foreign Languages Bookstore** (235 Wangfujing Dajie; daily 9am–9pm), with a selection of novels and children's books in English.

Beijing's newest high-end shopping district is centred around the Sanlitun embassy district. Taikoo Li draws crowds with flagship Adidas and Apple stores and clothes its shoppers with mid-priced labels such as American Apparel and The North Face. The newer and more luxurious Taikoo Li North has luxury brand Emporio Armani and domestic designers Brand New China and Eldi. South of the village is Sanlitun SOHO, a mixed-use residential and commercial development that is filling up slowly with shops and fine restaurants.

SHOPPING MALLS

At the southern end of Wangfujing Dajie, opposite Beijing Hotel, is **Oriental**, the city's premier shopping venue – a vast complex with boutiques, restaurants and cafés. Further north up Wangfujing Dajie, **Sun Dong An Plaza**, also known as Xin Dong An, is another enormous, multi-tiered shopping mall.

The **Lufthansa Centre Youyi Shopping City** (52 Liangmaqiao Lu; daily 9am–9pm), another upmarket mall, carries products with a broader price range. It stocks one of Beijing's best selections of silk by the metre at reasonable prices.

Several other modern and fashionable malls have opened over the past few years in Beijing. The **Peninsula Arcade** (8 Jinyu Hutong; daily 9am–9pm) and the **China World Shopping Mall** (1 Jianguomenwai Dajie; daily 9am–9pm), both upmarket malls, are filled with international designer brands.

Peking opera performer

ENTERTAINMENT

In a short time, Beijing has gone from a staid city, with lights out by 8pm, to a raucous party town. For a more subdued but no less vibrant experience, opt for performances of traditional opera or acrobatics.

If you want to do what most Beijingers do after the sun sets, the first place to go is where the food is: the night markets and restaurants. Night markets are fair-weather spots where you can sit outside, eat snacks and swill cool beer. If the weather is colder, seek out Mongolian hot pot, which epitomises the Chinese proverb of 'making one thing serve two purposes' by warming your hands as you cook your own dinner.

More 'formal' entertainments such as catching a show at a theatre are less popular with locals and it is usually the visiting foreign performers who create enough buzz to sell a decent amount of tickets. In recent years, several super-star performers of crosstalk – a type of comic dialogue that relies heavily on word-play – have emerged to fill houses, though the long-anticipated revival of Chinese performing arts has yet to be fully realised.

If all this seems overwhelming, the local English-language lifestyle magazines do an excellent job of picking out the best entertainment events of all types going on around town. Try The Beijinger (www.thebeijinger.com), Time Out Beijing (www.timeoutbeijing.com), City Weekend (www.cityweekend.com.cn) and That's Beijing (www.thatsmags.com) for updated listings.

Tickets for many cultural events in Beijing, including theatre, music, ballet and Peking opera, can be bought online from www.webtix.com.cn.

PEKING OPERA

Pop music may have captured the hearts of the masses, but there is a dedicated contingent of Peking opera fans who keep the art form alive. A word to the wise – if you're not yet sure if you like opera, go for the excerpts.

A sort of 'best of' Peking opera can be found at the Qianmen Hotel's **Liyuan Theatre** (175 Yong'an Lu; performances daily 7.30–8.45pm; tel: 6301 6688, ext. 8860). Designed for foreign visitors, and using English subtitles, it tends to choose action-packed martial stories, as well as excerpts from the classic novel *Journey to the West*. These are great fun because the characters wear colourful costumes and there are plenty of acrobatics to dramatise battles.

More 'serious' locations include **Chang'an Grand Theatre** (7 Jianguo-

The choice of drink is yours

mennei Dajie; tel: 6510 1310 ext. 10), Huguang Huiguan (3 Hufang Lu; tel: 6351 8284) and **Zhengyici Peking Opera Theatre** (see page 58). Call in advance to check performance times.

ACROBATICS

The sad truth about acrobatics is that many of the big shows staged in Beijing follow the same staid routines that have been around for hundreds of years. It is rare, therefore, to meet locals who are keen to take in a show. The skill level of Chinese acrobats is beyond question, however, and many of the performances attract healthy numbers of tourists. You can catch a standard, kitschy Chinese show at the **Chaoyang Theatre** (36 Dongsanhuan Beilu; tel: 6506 0838; daily 8.30am–8.30pm), with plate-spinning, contortionists and 11 girls stacked onto a single bicycle.

Chinese martial arts have long played a part in performance. **Red Theatre** (44 Xingfu Dajie; tel: 135 5252 7373) puts on a nightly show 'The Legend of Kung Fu' combining acting, acrobatics and a performer showing off his kung fu skills through such feats as breaking a metal bar across his forehead.

THEATRE

Ticket prices at major theatres in Beijing are still out of reach of ordinary people, making the entertainment scene rather dominated by tourists and wealthy locals. Things are changing, however, and grass-roots performances now take place in areas that attract arty types – such as the 798 Art District. Keen to make the controversial venue a success, the city government has been supporting the architecturally stunning **National Centre for the Performing Arts** (Chang'an Avenue; tel: 6655 0000; www.chncpa.org) in its ability to attract big-name international acts. Another option is the **Capital Theatre** (22 Wangfujing Dajie; tel: 6524 9847; www.bjry.com), a large, Soviet-style building and a premier venue for Chinese-language theatre and occasional performance space for visiting troupes from abroad.

CONCERTS

The China Philharmonic Orchestra chooses the **Poly Theatre** (14 Dongzhimen Nandajie; tel: 6500 1188) for its concerts. You can also enjoy varied shows here performed by groups from around China and Asia. The China National Orchestra's regular venue is the **Beijing Concert Hall** (1 Beixinhua Jie; tel: 6605 5812). MAO Livehouse (111 Gulou Dongdajie, 133 6612 1459, www.maolive.com) and Yugong Yishan (3-2 Zhang Zizhong Lu, 6404 2711, www.yugongyishan.com) are the city's top venues for local Chinese rock bands and touring alternative acts. Decent jazz can be seen at **East Shore**, which also boasts an unbeatable view over the Qianhai Lake as a backdrop.

A depiction of the Boxer Rebellion

HISTORY: KEY DATES

Beijing served as the imperial capital of China for over 1,000 years. After decades of turmoil under the Communists, the Deng era brought bold market reforms, and the ensuing economic growth continues even today.

EARLY HISTORY

1030–221 BC	The city of Ji develops on the site of Beijing.
221–207 BC	Emperor Qin Shi Huangdi unifies China.
200 BC–AD 1200	Beijing becomes a strategic garrison town between warring kingdoms.

THE MIDDLE AGES

1215	Mongols led by Genghis Khan overrun Beijing.
1260	Kublai Khan founds the Yuan dynasty.
1271	Kublai Khan establishes the capital of Dadu (Khan Balik) in Beijing. Marco Polo visits China.
1368–1644	The Ming dynasty.
1400s	The Forbidden City and most of the existing Great Wall are built.
1644–1911	The Qing dynasty.
1839–42	The First Opium War.
1860	The Second Opium War.
1861–1908	Empress Dowager Cixi holds power.

20TH CENTURY

1900	The Boxer Rebellion lays siege to the Foreign Legation Quarter.
1911	The revolution headed by Sun Yat-sen ends imperial rule.
1919	The Treaty of Versailles cedes territory to Japan and sparks the May Fourth Movement for democracy and sovereignty.
1921	The Communist Party of China is founded in Shanghai.
1935	Communists embark on the Long March.
1937	Full-scale invasion by the Japanese, who occupy much of China until the end of World War II.

The People's Liberation Army takes over Beijing in 1949

1949	Mao Zedong declares the People's Republic of China.
1957–59	Tiananmen Square and surrounding monoliths are built.
1957	The Anti-Rightist Movement singles out 300,000 intellectuals for criticism, punishment or imprisonment.
1958	Mao Zedong launches the disastrous Great Leap Forward.
1959–61	Great Leap Forward results in a famine that kills over 30 million.
1960	Beijing and Moscow split, beginning two decades of Cold War.
1966–76	The Cultural Revolution leads to widespread persecution, chaos and near economic collapse.
1972	President Nixon visits Beijing.
1976	Premier Zhou Enlai and Chairman Mao die.
1978	Premier Deng Xiaoping launches economic reforms.
1989	Tiananmen Square pro-democracy demonstrations are put down.
1993	China's parliament officially endorses market economy and begins a series of structural reforms.
1997	Deng Xiaoping dies. Hong Kong returns to China. President Jiang Zemin consolidates power.
1999	China celebrates the 50th anniversary of its founding. Macau returns to China.

21ST CENTURY

2001	China joins the World Trade Organization.
2003	Hu Jintao replaces Jiang Zemin as president; Wen Jiabao replaces Zhu Rongji as premier.
2008	The 29th Olympic Games are held in Beijing. China wins 51 gold medals. A $586 billion economic stimulus package for infrastructure and social welfare is announced.
2010	China becomes the world's second largest economy in terms of GDP.
2011	Fearful of the Middle East protests spreading to China, the government ramps up internet censorship and arrests dissidents including artist Ai Weiwei.
2013	Xi Jinping becomes president. He begins a massive anti-corruption campaign, imprisoning thousands of government officials – later including some of the political top brass.
2015	China's economic growth falls to its lowest level in almost 20 years.

BEST ROUTES

Enter the Forbidden City by the 'Upright Gate'

IMPERIAL BEIJING

First stop: the imperial heart of the city. See Beijing's most important sights, beginning with monumental Communist structures and the largest public square in the world, before taking a tour of the Forbidden City. End the day relaxing in the gardens of Coal Hill Park.

DISTANCE: 3.5km (2 miles)
TIME: A full day
START: Qianmen
END: Coal Hill Park
POINTS TO NOTE: Be sure to bring water and some food, as it takes hours to see the Forbidden City in detail and there are few refreshment choices available inside. To reach the starting point of the tour, take the subway to the Qianmen stop. You can also reach Tiananmen by taking the subway to either the Tian'anmen Xi or Tian'anmen Dong stop.

For over half a millennium, the Forbidden City was the cradle of imperial politics and administration, while Tiananmen Square was where major post-dynastic revolutionary events unfolded, a place of significance for both imperial and Communist history. Your first tour logically starts here at the heart of Beijing, where Chinese classical heritage and revolutionary symbolism converge.

SOUTH OF TIANANMEN SQUARE

Begin at **Qianmen** ❶ (Front Gate; daily 8.30am–4.30pm; charge), the largest of nine similar gates in the wall that used to embrace the Inner City, which has at its centre the Imperial Palace, also known as the Forbidden City. Qianmen, built in 1419, was initially used solely for the emperor's annual visits to the Temple of Heaven, where, after three days of fasting, he would pray for a good harvest. Residents outside the gate were forbidden to watch the procession, and had to keep their doors and windows sealed. Destroyed during the Boxer Rebellion of 1900, the gate was rebuilt in 1905. The front gate provides a great vantage point for studying the layout of old Beijing.

Qianmen is divided into two sections, which were once part of a single fortress-like complex. The northern section, across the street, is the main entrance of **Zhengyangmen** ('Facing the Sun' Gate), and the southern section is **Jianlou** (Arrow Tower), built in 1439

A detailed bronze urn   *Tiananmen Gate*

to serve as a watchtower. The Outer City, which was also enclosed by a high wall, extends southwards. Hard to ignore is the broad, pedestrianised shopping street Qianmen Dajie immediately south from which bustling, narrow streets to the south form the lively Dazhalan shopping district, which at the end of the 19th century teemed with decadent pleasures for off-duty officials. Further south is the Temple of Heaven.

Orientation

From Qianmen, you can get an overview of the imperial city. The north side of Qianmen overlooks Tiananmen Square, in the middle of which stands an obelisk, the Monument to the People's Heroes. To the left stands the Great Hall of the People, and to the right, the National Museum of China. In the centre of the square is the Mao Zedong Mausoleum.

At the far end of the square, across Dongchang'an Jie, is Tianan-

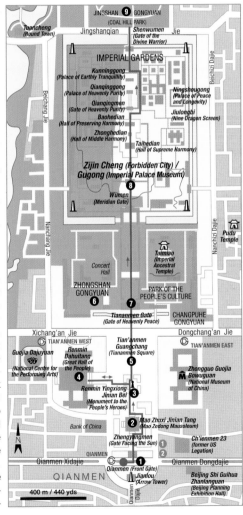

The grand Great Hall of the People

men Gate, the Gate of Heavenly Peace, leading the way to the Forbidden City, which is now officially known as the Palace Museum (Gugong). To the immediate west of Tiananmen Gate is the entrance to Zhongshan Park, dedicated to the early Nationalist leader Sun Yat-sen. The park used to be part of the Forbidden City, as did Zhongnanhai further west, where China's top leaders now live. To the northwest you can see the White Dagoba in Beihai Park, which was once part of the imperial gardens.

Before leaving Qianmen, visit the **photography exhibition** inside (daily 9am–4pm; charge). There are wonderful photographs of Beijing at the turn of the century, depicting scenes from cricket fighting to camel caravans arriving at the city gate.

Mao Zedong Mausoleum
Join the queue to pay your respects at the **Mao Zedong Mausoleum ❷** (Mao Zhuxi Jiniantang; Tue–Sun 8–11.30am, Aug–May also Tue, Thur 2–4pm; free), completed in 1977, a year after his death. Even today, when the little red book of Mao quotations is long past its sell-by date, people from all over China visit his mausoleum. You must leave your bag and camera at the door, or you will be turned away. Though the queue looks daunting, visitors are hustled through quickly. As you file past the preserved body of the Great Helmsman – one of the four

Grand Old Men of Marxism-Leninism who are lying in state – you are likely to ponder the rumours of body doubles, nightly deep-freezes and parts falling off the Chairman. But also be aware of the reverence paid by those around you.

Just outside the mausoleum, you get a graphic picture of how socialism is fast becoming mere consumer kitsch, as people are ushered through a small bazaar selling Chairman Mao busts, bags, badges and musical lighters playing *The East is Red*.

Monument to the People's Heroes
The 37m (121ft) obelisk that you saw earlier in the centre of Tiananmen Square is called the **Monument to the People's Heroes ❸** (Renmin Yingxiong Jinian Bei), dedicated in 1958 to those who died for the country. The bas-relief on the pedestal portrays the struggle from the First Opium War (1839–42) to the founding of the People's Republic of China (PRC) in 1949. Start on the east side and move clockwise to see it chronologically. During the 1989 student protests, this was the rallying point for the massive demonstrations.

Great Hall of the People
Next, visit the **Great Hall of the People ❹** (Renmin Dahuitang; daily 9am–5pm except during meetings; charge). Officially opened in 1959, this is where China's parliament, the National People's Congress, meets and other

Mao Zedong Mausoleum

The Egg

important conferences and diplomatic meetings take place. In the hall, there is one room dedicated to each of China's 32 provinces and regions. Across the square, another similarly imposing building houses the **National Museum of China** (Zhongguo Guojia Bowuguan; Tue–Sun 9am–5pm; free) which, following a four-year renovation, was opened in 2011 as the biggest museum in the world. A cavernous main hall is flanked by two wings boasting 65,000 sq m (700,000 sq ft) of exhibition space – one third of the entire floor area. Permanent exhibitions focus on Chinese arts, culture and, particularly, history. Though a godsend for students of ancient Chinese history, some of the tumultuous events of the 20th century have proved inconvenient to the Communist leadership and are notable by their absence.

TIANANMEN SQUARE

Relax for a while in **Tian'anmen Guangchang** ❺ (Tiananmen Square). In the Ming and Qing times, two rows of ministry offices stood on this site. When the emperor wanted to hand down an edict, he would pass with great fanfare to deliver it to the Ministry of Rites, where it was recopied and distributed throughout the empire.

Many buildings in the square were demolished to make it larger than any other public square in the world,

including Red Square in Moscow. For many Westerners, Tiananmen Square is synonymous with the democracy demonstrations of 1989, but for most Chinese, it conjures up a wider range of images, both dark and joyous. Since the end of imperial times, the plaza has been at the heart of Chinese politics. In the spring of 1919, May Fourth protesters gathered here to demand that their government reform itself and the nation. Thirty years later on 1 October 1949, hundreds of thou-

---

The Egg

For a glimpse of a new kind of national monument, make a detour around the northern end of the Great Hall of the People to the National Centre for the Performing Arts, formerly known as the China National Grand Theatre. This enormous edifice, disparagingly nicknamed 'The Egg', has been received with scepticism by most Beijing residents for being too grandiose, for ignoring the principles of *feng shui*, and for clashing with its surroundings. The grand theatre has since struggled to deliver high art to the masses or truly bring about a renaissance of the local Peking opera, though it proves a popular spot for moat-side strolls (particularly when illuminated at night) and an entrance ticket is an inexpensive way to marvel at its interior and view displays in the exhibition areas.

A portrait of Chairman Mao graces Tiananmen Gate

sands of cheering soldiers and citizens convened here to hear Mao Zedong declare the founding of the PRC from atop Tiananmen Gate. During the Cultural Revolution in the 1960s, Red Guards held their near-hysterical gatherings here.

Today, Tiananmen Square is mostly packed with domestic tourists marvelling at the collection of extravagant monuments that form the centre of their nation's great capital. A flag-raising and lowering ceremony is performed by PLA soldiers in the north of the square daily at sunrise and sunset.

Though this may be the centre of the city, the food situation here is sorely lacking. Besides streetside vendors, two restaurants, **Quanjude**, see ❶, and **Donglaishun**, see ❷, are practically the only choices. The smartest option may be to visit the Qianmen neighbourhood at the start of the day and stock up on local snacks for later. Don't forget bottled water. Save this food for the Forbidden City, which has only one, overpriced, café.

Zhongshan Park

If it is a warm day or if you are not up for the Forbidden City, **Zhongshan Park** ❻ (Zhongshan Gongyuan; daily 6am–9pm; charge) makes for a lovely detour. Originally the Altar of Land and Grain, where the emperor would pray and sacrifice for good harvests, it was made into a public park in 1914. The body of Sun Yat-sen (Sun Zhongshan in Mandarin) was placed here briefly after his death in 1925, and from 1928 the park took his name. It now houses some exquisite botanical exhibitions and the Forbidden City Concert Hall, one of the best in the city.

Tiananmen Gate

After lunch, return to the **Tiananmen Gate** ❼, the Gate of Heavenly Peace (daily 8.30am–5pm; free to pass, charge to ascend), to enter the Forbidden City. The gate, built in 1417 and restored in 1651, was where emperors made their first offerings on their way from the Forbidden City to the Temple of Heaven for New Year rites. There are five passages through the massive gate walls, of which the central one follows the imperial route and was reserved for the emperor. Today, it is open to all.

Tiananmen Gate is now adorned with Mao's gigantic portrait and the slogans 'Long live the People's Republic of China' and 'Long live the great union of the peoples of the world'. It was here that Chairman Mao announced the founding of the PRC before a crowd of 300,000 in 1949.

FORBIDDEN CITY

From Tiananmen Gate, a long approach takes you through a second gate before reaching the **Forbidden City** ❽ (Zijin Cheng; daily, Apr–Oct 8.30am–5pm, Nov–Mar 8.30am–4.30pm; charge), also called Imperial Palace or referred

Palace architectural details　　　　　　　　　　　　　　　　　*Marching guards*

to by its official Chinese name of Palace Museum (Gugong). A useful and informative audio guide, available in eight languages, can be rented. The audio guide can be collected as you enter the Forbidden City through the glass doors to the right of the main entrance.

The approach to the Forbidden City has now become a bit of a circus, with vendors, souvenir photographers and people who insist on leading you to see their 'art gallery'. The latter typically approach in pairs, and try to take visitors to a nearby room where hasty sketches are sold at very high prices. Some of the flanking buildings do house sights of interest, however; the exhibitions of Qing-dynasty photographs are worth seeing.

History
Behind walls more than 10m (30ft) high and within the 50m (160ft) long moat, life in the palace was dictated by complex rules and rituals. Entrance was denied to ordinary people, but today's tourists can easily access this fascinating display of Chinese cultural history in what is probably the best-preserved site of classical Chinese architecture.

In 1421, after 17 years of construction, the Ming emperor Yongle moved into the palace. Up until the founding of the republic in 1911 – a period covering the reign of 24 emperors from the Ming dynasty until the last emperor of the Qing dynasty, Puyi – the Forbidden City was the imperial residence and the cen-

tre of the Middle Kingdom. It has 9,000 rooms in which an estimated 8,000 to 10,000 people lived, including 3,000 eunuchs, as well as maids and concubines, all within an area of 70 hectares (180 acres).

The Forbidden City lay abandoned until the mid 1980s. Protected by the army during the Cultural Revolution, it was largely ignored in the years after, in part due to a faint popular superstition that deterred 'commoners' from visiting the former Imperial Palace. Rare photos of the area depict a remarkable site of antiquity and decrepitude, with crumbled bricks and grass growing rampant in the courtyards. More recent repair projects have revived old building techniques. Wooden structures are built using mortise and tenon instead of nails, and paint is applied using silk rags, not brushes. A peculiar technique is also used to make the so-called 'gold bricks' and paving stones, such that when these bricks are struck, a metallic sound is produced.

Layout and palace details
Currently, around two-thirds of the palace grounds are restored and open to the public. The entire site can be divided into two main areas: **Waichao**, the Outer Court in the south comprising three large halls where emperors held state cermonies; and **Neiting**, the Inner Residence in the rear, with three large palaces and a few smaller ones as

well as the imperial gardens. Through the middle of the site runs the imperial walkway, which is decorated with finely carved stone phoenix and dragon bas-reliefs, representing the empress and the emperor, respectively.

Among the details to look out for are the lion door guards, symbolising strength and dignity. On the right is usually a male lion pawing a ball, which is thought to represent the world. On the left, you often find a female with a cub under her paw. At the corners of most roofs are a parade of creatures often led by a man riding a hen. These were believed to discourage lightning from striking. Vast bronze urns are placed at regular intervals throughout the palace, and were once kept filled with water in case of fire, the greatest danger the palace faced.

Colours and numerology also have special significance. The yellow of the palace roof stands for the Earth; red walls represent fire, luck and happiness; blue and green mean spring and rebirth. Nine is a lucky number, reflected in the number of dragons on ramps and gold studs on doors.

Three great halls

Approaching from the **Meridian Gate** (Wumen), you see the three great halls and courtyards of the outer area. The **Hall of Supreme Harmony** (Taihedian) is the largest building in the palace, and also the first and most impressive of these. In its centre is the ornately carved golden **Dragon Throne**, from which the emperor ruled. Only he could enter the hall by walking up the ramp adorned with dragon motifs. On the platform in front of the hall are two symbols: a grain measure on the left and a sundial to the right, which represent agriculture and imperial justice, respectively. Solemn ceremonies, such as the enthronement of a new emperor, were held in this hall. The courtyard could hold 90,000 spectators.

The **Hall of Middle Harmony** (Zhonghedian) is behind the Hall of Supreme Harmony. This was where the emperor prepared for ceremonies before entering the main hall. On display here is an imperial palanquin. The **Hall of Preserving Harmony** (Baohedian) was used for examinations and lavish banquets. These two halls complete a trinity that reflects the Three Buddhas and the Three Pure Ones of Taoism. To the east of the Hall of Preserving Harmony is the magnificent **Nine Dragon Screen** (Jiulongbi).

Palace of Peace and Longevity

Facing the Nine Dragon Screen is the **Palace of Peace and Longevity** (Ningshougong). The last emperor Puyi lived in the palace until 1925, despite the founding of the republic in 1911. In 1932, he became the puppet emperor of Manchukuo, the Japanese-occupied territory in northeast China. Many palace treasures were stolen by the Japanese or taken

Nine Dragon Screen

to Taiwan by fleeing Nationalists, but the smaller halls to the east and the west of the main halls still contain the impressive collections of the Forbidden City. A highlight is the clock and jewellery hall, with water clocks and ornate mechanical clocks.

Palace of Heavenly Purity

On the other side of the imposing Outer Court, to the north and separated by the **Gate of Heavenly Purity** (Qianqingmen), lies a labyrinth of gates, doors, pavilions, gardens and palaces. This is called the **Palace of Heavenly Purity** (Qianqinggong), the residence of the imperial family, who were almost all exclusively female; the emperor and eunuchs were the only men permitted to enter. The male members of the emperor's family lived in prince's residences (*wangfu*, as in Wangfujing, see page 34) scattered around the city, which were generally palatial in their own right.

COAL HILL PARK

After dropping off your audio guide near the **Gate of the Divine Warrior** (Shenwumen), the north gate of the Imperial Palace, cross Jingshan Qianjie to **Coal Hill Park** ❾ (Jingshan Gongyuan; daily 6am–9pm; charge). This is the best place to appreciate the sheer scale of the palace complex, particularly at night when spotlights are trained on the corner towers. The artificial hill was

built with the earth dug from the palace moats in the early 15th century. In Qing emperor Qianlong's day, the park was stocked with deer, rabbits and songbirds. The last Ming emperor, Chongzhen, fled the besieged Forbidden City and hanged himself from a tree on the hill in 1644. A new tree has been planted on the same spot to record the event for posterity.

Food and drink

❶ QUANJUDE

44 Dongjiaomin Xiang (south-eastern corner of Tiananmen Square); tel: 6512 2265; daily 11am–8pm; $$
Another branch of Beijing's most famous Peking duck outlet; due to its location, this one is slightly more expensive than the others.

❷ DONGLAISHUN

44 Dongjiaomin Xiang (south-eastern corner of Tiananmen Square); tel: 6524 1042; daily 11am–8.30pm; $$
This hot-pot chain, first opened in 1903, is famous for the quality of its meat. *Shuanyangrou* is lamb dipped in boiling water, though in most restaurants the meat needs to be cooked for quite some time. Donglaishun's tender, thin sliced lamb, however, can literally be 'dipped' in the pot, then straight in the savoury sesame sauce. This is truly some of the best meat in the city.

Bustling crowd on Wangfujing Food Street

WANGFUJING AND THE FOREIGN LEGATION QUARTER

Stroll through Beijing's main shopping street and then take a leisurely walk or cycle through the former Legation Quarter, a fascinating piece of preserved history where foreign diplomats lived at the turn of the last century.

DISTANCE: 2.5km (1.5 miles)
TIME: 2.5 hours
START: Oriental Plaza
END: Beijing Hotel
POINTS TO NOTE: Take the subway to the Wangfujing stop, from where you can walk to Oriental Plaza.

The name Wangfujing dates back to the Yuan dynasty. Then it was called Wangfu Street, after a prince's residence that was located here. The name was changed later in the Ming dynasty when a well (*jing*) was discovered. By the late Qing dynasty the street was a major commercial thoroughfare and many of Beijing's age-old brand names can still be found here.

WANGFUJING STREET

At the southern end of **Wangfujing Dajie** (Wangfujing Street) is the vast **Oriental Plaza ❶** shopping complex, a mandatory shopping experience that is also home to one of Beijing's fin-

est hotels, the **Grand Hyatt Beijing**. Peruse the complex at your leisure and then stroll north up Wangfujing Dajie, past the huge Wangfujing Bookstore, perhaps diving left into the **Wangfujing Xiaochijie** (Wangfujing Food Street). Marked by a decorated archway, this busy quarter teems with small restaurants and stalls serving dishes from all over China. About 100m/yds

Oriental Plaza   *Wangfujing shopping street*

to the north, on the west side of the street, is the **Wangfujing Foreign Languages Bookstore** (tel: 8080 8383; daily 9.30am–4.30pm), one of the best spots in the city for books in English. While the prices are comparable to what you would pay in a bookstore in America or Europe, the selection is fantastic. Be wary: Wangfujing is a prime location for scams against foreigners, which usually begin with a pretty girl or two asking to practice their English or take you to their art gallery. Be friendly, but firm.

ST JOSEPH'S CATHEDRAL

Head north 500m/yds to one of Beijing's most recognisable Catholic monuments, **St Joseph's Cathedral ❷** (Dongtang). St Joseph's was originally built in 1655 by the Qing emperor Shunzhi for resident Jesuits, and has since symbolised the presence of the West in China under many different circumstances. It was damaged or destroyed countless times over the past few centuries – by earthquake in 1720, fire in 1812 and the Boxer Rebellion in 1900. It now serves an active congregation of foreign and Chinese worshippers, though like all Catholic churches in China it is not recognised by the Vatican. It is also a favourite setting for newlyweds and wedding photographers: its grand exterior and flocks

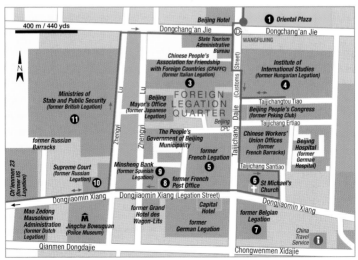

Wrought-iron gate of the former Italian Legation

of pigeons create the perfect atmosphere for brides and grooms looking to convey a sense of Europe. On nice days, three or four couples can be seen vying for good spots.

FOREIGN LEGATION QUARTER

Early 20th-century European architecture in China is an instant reminder of the ignominious decline of the Qing dynasty and the foreign domination that followed. The **Foreign Legation Quarter**, south of Oriental Plaza and east of Tiananmen Square, contains many elegant European buildings that recall part of modern China's history. Between the 1860s and the outbreak of the Sino–Japanese War in 1937, 13 foreign governments were represented here, their presence forced on the Chinese by the outcome of the Opium Wars. Diplomats were living here up until the communists reclaimed the property in 1949: they had their own administration, police, churches, hospitals, shops and post office, guarded by some 1,000 soldiers. In 1900, during the Boxer Rebellion, which was raging over much of northern China, the Foreign Legation Quarter was a main target. The area was shelled for a month or more, much of it flattened in the process. After the rebellion was put down, in part by foreign armies, diplomats more or less had a free hand exacting revenge on the former Boxers. Furthermore, the legation quarter was rebuilt and fortified with its own version of a city wall, and closed off to Chinese nationals.

Former Italian Legation

To get to the Foreign Legation Quarter, backtrack south to Oriental Plaza, cross over Dongchang'an Jie and head down Taijichang Dajie (Customs Street). About 200m/yds along on the right, at No. 1, you come to the gate of the **former Italian Legation ❸**, where the Italians relocated to in 1900 after the Boxer rebels destroyed their previous quarters. It now houses the Chinese People's Association for Friendship with Foreign Countries (CPAFFC).

Former Hungarian Legation

Continue along Taijichang Dajie but cross to the opposite side. Walk alongside a high grey wall topped with curved tiles and turn left into the first alleyway. About 200m/yds on the left is the **former Hungarian Legation ❹**, which is now the Institute of International Studies. Built in 1900, the simple grey-and-white building changed hands many times. In 1915, when China declared war on Germany and its allies, the building was occupied by the Hungarians. After a short spell under the Dutch, a Russian general turned it into a guesthouse in the late 1920s. In 1938, it became the German Club. The Americans used it for the Allied Property Administration and it later became the Hungarian Embassy. The building was finally returned to the Chinese in 1969.

St Michael's Church   *The leafy Foreign Legation Quarter*

Double back to Taijichang Dajie and turn left. Through the first gate on the left is an elegant grey-blue building with arches along the ground floor, topped by a red national emblem and a single portal. This is the headquarters of the **Beijing People's Congress** (closed to the public). Built in 1902, it was once the Peking Club, with a swimming pool and tennis courts that were still in use as late as the 1960s. The white building opposite, topped with an enormous red star, is the headquarters of the Communist Party Committee of the Beijing municipality.

Former French Legation

Moving along Taijichang Dajie, you enter 'Little France'. The French, along with the British, were the first to install permanent diplomatic representatives here. They held large tracts of land on both sides of the street. On the right side of the street are the graceful rooflines of the **former French Legation ❺**. Turn left at the second alleyway, Taijichang Santiao, about 200m/yds beyond the Peking Club. French theologian Teilhard de Chardin, who lived in China from 1932 to 1946, founded an institute of geobiology on this street. Much of this area has been replaced with typical Chinese apartment blocks, but about 100m/yds along on the left, you can peer through the gates of the **former French Barracks**. The Soviet-style building in the centre is now Chinese Workers' Union offices.

St Michael's Church

Continue for another 100m/yds along Taijichang Santiao and turn right. After another 100m/yds, you come to Dongjiaomin Xiang (Legation Street). Turn right again. Just before the next junction, about 200m/yds along on the right, is **St Michael's Church ❻**, an intimate little neo-Gothic church built by the French Vincentian Order in 1902. St Michael's was closed after the 1949 revolution, but was renovated and reopened in 1989. Services are held daily, and the staff and congregants are happy to let you stroll through to visit or pray. The figures of the saints above the chapel doors date all the way back to 1889 and some of the stained glass and ceramic tiles are original too.

Former Belgian Legation

Opposite the church, you can see the jagged brick rooflines and green tops of the **former Belgian Legation ❼**, originally modelled after a villa of King Leopold II. Before 1900, this was the home of a high-level Chinese official, Xu Tong, who hated foreigners so much that he purportedly wished to cover his sedan chair with their skin. He did his best to avoid them, but when the European Allied Armies entered Beijing in 1900 in reaction to the Boxer Rebellion, Xu Tong could take it no longer. He committed suicide.

From St Michael's Church, cross Taijichang Dajie and continue along

Standing guard outside the Belgian Legation

Dongjiaomin Xiang. About 50m/yds past the junction, where two massive stone lions and two armed soldiers stand guard, are the red gates of another building belonging to the former French Legation. This is the former occasional residence of Cambodian King Norodom Sihanouk, a favour from the Chinese government when he went into exile.

Across the road are the **former offices of Jardine Matheson**, one of the earliest Western trading companies in Asia. About 200m/yds further along on Dongjiaomin Xiang on the right, a tiny building with fancy brickwork, a zigzag roofline and arched windows now houses the authentically spicy Sichuan restaurant Jingyuan Chuancai (tel: 6524 4156; daily 10.30am–2pm, 6.30–9.30pm). This was originally the **French Post Office** ❽ and also the site of the original Beijing Hotel before it moved to its current location in 1900.

Former Spanish Legation

Next to the French Post Office is the **former Spanish Legation** ❾, where the protocol on the Boxer Rebellion was signed in 1901. The Spanish sold the corner lot to the Yokohama Specie Bank. Currently, the building houses Minsheng Bank. Empress Dowager Cixi was said to have borrowed money here just before the last dynasty fell. The valuables she put up as collateral were never reclaimed and are now

in a collection in London. The bank stands on the corner of Dongjiaomin Xiang and Zhengyi Lu, the divided north–south street. 'Zhengyi' means 'justice', but the road used to be called Canal Street when it served as the Forbidden City's sewage outflow. It was filled in in 1925 to create the promenade between the two lanes.

Former Russian Legation

Cross Zhengyi Lu and continue on Dongjiaomin Xiang. On the right was once the site of the Russian Orthodox Mission, and was later the **Russian Legation** ❿ and then the Soviet Legation. Russian Orthodox priests were some of the first foreigners to move into the area, well before it became a recognised neighbourhood for foreign representatives. Until 1991, there was a simple stone building here, probably the former Russian church. The expanded Supreme Court now stands here.

Opposite it is the **Police Museum** (Jingcha Bowuguan; Tue–Sun 9am–4pm; charge), showcasing the history of China's police force, forensic methods and an impressively comprehensive collection of old-fashioned torture devices. About 300m/yds further down on the left side of the street is a brick structure with a green roof. The **former Dutch Legation**, it is now the office of the Mao Zedong Mausoleum Administration. On the right is the former American legation com-

The former Spanish Legation   *The stoic former Dutch Legation*

pound, now a luxurious but troubled modern development, Chi'enmen 23 (tel: 6522 4848; daily 9am–6pm). This ambitious 'lifestyle development' has struggled to retain lesees but can still boast the Yunnanese restaurant **Lost Heaven**, see ①, and the lavish whiskey bar **Johnnie Walker House Beijing**, see ②, as well as a large art exhibition space.

Backtrack on Dongjiaomin Xiang and make a left turn onto Zhengyi Lu for the final stretch. The area on the right side of Zhengyi Lu, north of Minsheng Bank, was the **former Japanese Legation** where the Chinese were forced to accept the infamous 'Twenty-One Demands' on 7 May 1915, whereby the Japanese obtained special rights over Manchuria. It now houses the Beijing mayor's office and the offices of the city government.

Former British Legation

The last, and possibly grandest relic on this walk is further along Zhengyi Lu on the left: the former **British Legation ⑪**. Previously a prince's palace, this building was the city's largest foreign legation. The British moved in after the Second Opium War of 1860 and expanded the area to create the largest territory held by foreigners. Many sought refuge here during the siege of 1900. They retained this compound until 1959, but it is now occupied by the Ministries of State and Public Security – the Chinese version of the KGB.

The grand gateway of the legation had housed a tiny shop for 10 years or so, and its enormous coat of arms was moved to London. The building has now been refitted with grand doors and put back into service.

The Legation loop brings you to the northern end of Zhengyi Lu and onto Dongchang'an Jie, across from the Beijing Hotel.

Food and drink

① LOST HEAVEN

Chi'enmen 23, 23 Qianmen Dongdajie; tel: 8516 2698; daily 11.30am–2pm; 5.30–10.30pm; $$

The Beijing branch of the popular Shanghai chain transports diners to the jungles and mountains of southwest China, with an impressive selection of fragrant minority dishes. Book ahead for a second-floor terrace seat to enjoy an excellent view of the compound.

② JOHNNIE WALKER HOUSE BEIJING

Chi'enmen 23, 23 Qianmen Dongdajie; tel: 6526 0609; Tue–Sun 9am–noon; $$$

Described by the company as the world's largest embassy for Scotch whiskey outside of Scotland, the bar of this ultra-luxury private club is a classy love letter to the spirit (and the brand).

Worshippers at the Lama Temple

LAMA TEMPLE, CONFUCIUS TEMPLE AND DITAN PARK

A tour of two temples with different philosophical traditions – Lamaist Buddhism and Confucianism. Round out with dinner and then dancing in Ditan Park, a favourite recreational playground of Beijing residents.

DISTANCE: 1km (0.6 mile)
TIME: Half a day, from early afternoon
START: Lama Temple
END: Peony Garden
POINTS TO NOTE: Take the subway to the Yonghegong stop. The sights are all within a 1km (0.6-mile) radius, so this is an easy walk.

Buddhism arrived in China from India in the 1st century, but Lamaism, the sect of Tibetan Buddhism that incorporates shamanist beliefs and practices, gained influence only after the Mongolians conquered Tibet and China in the 13th century. The Mongolian rulers had close relationships with Tibetan Buddhist leaders, and this led to the spread of Lamaism throughout China. During the Qing dynasty, Lamaism's influence was revived by the Manchus, who also practised the faith.

LAMA TEMPLE

Originally the private residence of Prince Yong, the **Lama Temple** ❶ (Yonghegong; daily 9am–4pm; charge) was turned into a monastery after its owner became Emperor Yongzheng in 1723. The golden roof tiles, restricted to imperial residences and temples are a remnant of its days under its former tenant. According to custom, the former residence of a Son of Heaven had to be dedicated to religious purposes once he left. Hence in 1744, Yongzheng's son, Emperor Qianlong, established it as a monastery and it soon flourished as a centre of Lamaist religion and art. At the same time, it offered the Qing rulers welcome opportunities for influencing and controlling their Tibetan and Mongolian subjects.

The temple, the most elaborately restored sacred building in Beijing, belongs to the Yellow Hat sect, though many traditional characteristics of that sect are missing. The monks do not wear yellow hats, for instance, or even the red robes common to Tibetan Buddhist lamas. This may have something to do with the sect's spiritual leader, the Dalai Lama. Since the Chinese invasion of Tibet in 1950, relations between the authorities and Buddhist leaders have

Drum and stele at the temple   *Golden Roof*

been problematic. The current Dalai Lama fled to India in 1959 after failing to win independence for Tibet. He is still condemned by Beijing, but his image, once forbidden, can now be displayed in temples. The government officially remains atheist, but with the reforms since 1978, churches and temples have been restored, along with the right to worship. Now the neighbourhood around the Lama Temple caters to the Buddhist faithful – statuary and religious items are sold in shops along Yonghegong Dajie, and the smell of incense wafts through the streets.

Pavilion of 10,000 Happinesses

Today, about 70 monks live in the Lama Temple. Its five halls and three gates are laid out along a north-south axis. In each successive hall, the central Buddha is more imposing than the last. In the three-storeyed section of the fifth hall, the **Pavilion of Ten Thousand Happinesses** (Wanfuge), is a 23m (75ft) high statue of the Buddha carved from a single piece of sandalwood – recognized by the Guinness Book of World Records in 1993 as the largest of its kind in the world. It took three years to transport the piece of sandalwood used for the statue from Nepal to Beijing; the building that houses the statue was built after it was completed.

Lamaism's roots lie in the mysterious rituals of the ancient Tibetan Bön religion. Look closely at the carvings and Tibetan *thangka* paintings in the side halls. One image shows the goddess Lamo riding a horse cloaked in the skin

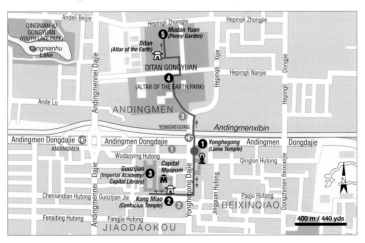

Stele collection at the Confucius Temple

of her own son, who was sacrificed to show her detachment from the world.

CONFUCIUS TEMPLE

Your next stop is the **Confucius Temple** ❷ (Kongzi Miao; daily 9am–4.30pm; charge), a tranquil former centre of scholarship. Go west on Guozijian Jie, the street opposite the Lama Temple across Yonghegong Dajie. The entrance to the Confucius Temple is 200m/yds on the right.

In the Confucius Temple's glorious past, emperors came to offer sacrifices to Confucius at the **Hall of Great Achievement**, hoping for guidance in governance. Confucius was a teacher in the state of Lu (in present-day Shandong province) in the 6th century BC, about the same time the Buddha was teaching in India. The brand of Confucianism adopted by the emperors stressed order and so Confucianism was an important tool for keeping order across the vast and diverse nation. Interestingly enough, that aspect of Confucianism is currently enjoying somewhat of a revival.

Built in 1306 during the Yuan dynasty, this is the second-largest Confucian temple in China, after the one in Qufu, Confucius' hometown. The temple courtyard is filled with ancient pines, most of them several hundred years old. Combined with the ancient structures, they give one sense of visiting the past. The temple's prized possession is a collection of 190 steles inscribed with records of ancient civil service examinations.

IMPERIAL ACADEMY

Leave the temple, turn right and walk 200m/yds along Guozijian Jie for a brief look at the former **Imperial Academy** ❸ (Guozijian; daily 8.30am–5pm; charge), now the Capital Library. Once the highest educational institution in the land, it was where thousands of students and scholars came to listen to emperors expound Confucian classics. A set of steles commissioned by the Qing emperor Qianlong records 13 Confucian classics. Its 800,000 characters were engraved by a single scholar over 12 years.

If you are interested in traditional Chinese handicrafts, browse the row of small shops at the far end of the Imperial Academy or along Guozijian Jie.

For refreshments, the burgeoning Wudaoying Hutong just west of the Lama Temple offers a number of bars and cafés including the reliable **Vineyard Café**, see ❶. A Buddhist-style vegetarian meal can be had at the popular **Xuxiangzhai Vegetarian Restaurant**, see ❷, across the street from the Confucius Temple. If it's already dinnertime, consider making a worthwhile trip south to night-time food street Gui Jie.

The landmark **Jin Ding Xuan**, see ❸, next to the entrance of Ditan Park, serves tasty dim sum at very reasonable prices 24-hours a day.

Confucius statue

Biyong Hall at the Imperial Academy

DITAN PARK

After dinner, proceed to **Ditan Park** ❹ (Ditan Gongyuan; daily 6am–9pm; charge). From Yonghegong Jie, walk north under Erhuan Lu (Second Ring Road). The south entrance is 300m/yds north of the Yonghegong subway station. **Ditan** (Altar of the Earth; daily 8am–5pm; charge) was first built in 1530 and had a similar ritual function as the Temple of Heaven. Each year, on the summer solstice during the Ming and Qing dynasties, the emperor came here to make sacrifices to the Earth God. The altar, a round platform surrounded by two concentric square walls where the sacrifices were offered, was restored in the 1980s. Beijing residents come to Ditan Park in the early morning to dance and exercise.

PEONY GARDEN

After exploring the park, join in one of the most popular pastimes of modern China – ballroom dancing. Dance parties are held daily (May–Oct 6.30–11am and 7–10pm, Nov–May 6.30–11am; charge) in **Peony Garden** ❺ (Mudan Yuan), 200m/yds north of the altar. The park officially closes at 9pm but the gate is open all night to accommodate dancers. The park also holds one of Beijing's best Spring Festival temple fairs, with performances including Peking opera, folk dancing and re-enactments of Qing-dynasty imperial rituals, as well as stalls selling traditional snacks.

Food and drink

❶ VINEYARD CAFÉ

31 Wudaoying Hutong; tel: 6402-7961; 11.30am–11.30pm; $
Well-known local eatery famed for its salads, frothy cappuccinos and decent wine list.

❷ XUXIANGZHAI VEGETARIAN RESTAURANT

26 Guozijian Dajie; tel: 6404-6568; daily 11.30am–2pm and 5.30–9pm; $$
There is a grand tradition in Beijing of Buddhist vegetarian restaurants, many of which serve 'mock meat' – sausage, duck, fish and chicken – which is made with tofu and other vegetable products, and surprisingly convincing. Xuxiangzhai gets extra credibility for its proximity to the Lama Temple, but really, it is the all-you-can-eat lunch buffets that make it popular.

❸ JIN DING XUAN

South gate of Ditan Park; tel: 6429 6888; daily 24 hours; $$
It is almost enough just to look at Jing Din Xuan from a distance: the vast, three-storey restaurant features giant red lanterns and swooping blue roofs. A renao (boisterous) atmosphere is guaranteed inside and the wide range of dim sum is satisfying and inexpensive, if not the most authentic in town.

Swimming in Houhai in autumn

THE LAKE DISTRICT

Once the pleasure ground of royalty, the Lake District now draws strollers and swimmers, as well as drinkers to its hip bars and cafés. Begin with a visit to the Drum and Bell towers, then snake your way around picturesque lakes to the imperial gardens of Beihai Park and Jade Island.

DISTANCE: 4km (2.5 miles)
TIME: Half a day. This tour is designed for the afternoon, but can easily be adapted for the morning.
START: Drum and Bell towers
END: Beihai Park
POINTS TO NOTE: Take a taxi to the Drum and Bell towers, or walk south from the Gulou subway stop. This whole area is very pleasant to walk through; cycling is also an excellent option.

The Lake District comprises Beihai Park, the former lakeside pleasure ground of the imperial family, and the Shicha-hai area, where a few other smaller 'back lakes' used to be the locale of many courtyard residences of Manchu princes and officials.

BELL AND DRUM TOWERS

Begin your tour at the grey **Bell Tower ❶** (Zhonglou) and the red **Drum Tower ❷** (Gulou; both daily 9am–4.30pm; charge).

Kublai Khan had the original towers built nearby to serve as the imperial clock. The Drum Tower held 24 giant drums, which were beaten to mark the closing of the city gates and the passing of the night watches. The bell in the Bell Tower was struck to announce the time of day. If you're hungry, stop at **Hani Gejiu**, see ❶.

The towers were replaced in 1420 during the Ming dynasty. The Bell Tower, which was made of wood, was burned down and then rebuilt of stone in 1747. Structurally, the 33m (108ft) high Bell Tower is more interesting. Its stone staircase leads through a dark passageway reminiscent of medieval castles. In 1990, the bell was reinstalled in the tower. Since then the mayor has climbed the tower every Spring Festival to ring in the Lunar New Year. A chief attraction of the Drum Tower is the view from the top of the surrounding area of traditional courtyard houses. In the hall at the top is an original drum, damaged during the Opium Wars, and a full set of replicas, which can be beaten by curious sightseers. The courtyard between the two towers is perfect for lingering

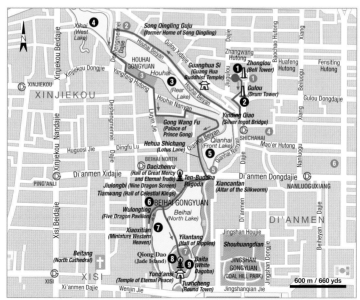

The bell in the Bell Tower   *Pedicab tour around the Lake District*

on a summer afternoon. Many pedicab tours also leave from here.

SURROUNDING HUTONG

Though this authentic and unrestored part of old Beijing constantly faces the threat of being bulldozed in the name of progress, it is, for now, a great place to explore. Zhangwang Hutong's history dates back to the Yuan dynasty and boasts two famous former residences: that of Reginald Johnston, the man who taught English to Emperor Puyi, and Princess Temple, once owned by

an eunuch who served Empress Cixi. Leading to **Nan Luogu Xiang** is Mao'er Hutong, one of the best-preserved *hutong* in Beijing. Its most famous distinguished resident was Wan Rong, last empress of China, who lived at No. 37 before marrying into the royal family. You can sneak into the central courtyard down a path to see the original supporting pillars and eaves. East of the Drum Tower stretches Gulou Dongdajie, packed with Chinese hipsters browsing vintage clothing boutiques, instrument shops and kitschy eateries. North of the avenue are the alleys criss-crossing

Taking it easy by the lake

Bei Luogu Xiang and Baochao Hutong, areas that despite a growing influx of chic coffee houses and bars still manage to show signs of an older, more traditional way of life.

Nanluogu Xiang

A detour worth making is Nanluogu Xiang – just follow Mao'er Hutong east from Di'anmen Dajie. It's one of the best shopping streets in town for quirky Chinese contemporary and retro gifts and clothes. Many of its shops are barely bigger than a large cupboard. There are also varied styles of cafés, bars and restaurants including neighbourhood mainstay Passerby Bar, see.

HOUHAI

Start your walk around the Shichahai lakes, comprising Houhai, Xihai and Qianhai. The Shichahai lake system is man-made; during the Yuan dynasty it connected with reservoirs further north to supply the capital with water.

From the Drum and Bell towers, head south on Di'anmen Dajie and turn right into the first alleyway you come to, about 50m/yds along. This is **Yandai Xiejie**, which has become a major part of the **Houhai ❸** (Rear Lake) scene, packed with tiny café-bars and knick-knack shops. Another 150m/yds along is a junction where you should make a left turn. Ahead is a stone bridge called **Silver Ingot Bridge** (Yinding Qiao), which divides Houhai from Qianhai (Front

Lake). The two are part of a string of six lakes extending all the way from the north to the south of the old Inner City.

This area of town was home to princes and wealthy, powerful families during the Qing dynasty, hence the larger-than-average courtyard homes. During the early years of the PRC, the spacious homes were divided up among many families, as happened all over the city. The neighbourhood was then mostly ignored until the SARS epidemic in 2003. Convinced that the secluded area was somehow safer as the restaurants and bars are outdoors, people began flocking here, leading to the establishment of a new bar area and the explosive growth that characterises the area today. Once again, wealthy people are buying the old courtyard homes and remodelling them, slowly restoring the neighbourhood to its historical character (albeit with the addition of neon).

If it is a nice day and you would like to stay by the lake, consider heading north from Silver Ingot Bridge. On the east edge of Houhai is the **Guang Hua Buddhist Temple** (Guanghua Si; daily 8am–4pm; charge). Constructed during the Yuan dynasty, it is now home to the Beijing Buddhist Society. Relatively modest in size, it is well preserved and stocked with the usual colourful array of Buddhist statues and artefacts.

On the north-eastern edge of Houhai is the **former residence of Song Qingling** (Song Qingling Guju; daily 9am–4pm; charge), the wife of Sun

View of Qianhai   *Silver Ingot Bridge*

Yat-sen. Song Qingling moved into the house in 1963 and lived there until her death in 1981. The guest room contains an exhibition of photographs, documents and objects from her life: her pampered Shanghai childhood as a daughter of one of China's most prominent families; her year as a student, her marriage to Sun Yat-sen, and her political activities and support for the resistance to Japanese occupation.

Worth seeking out is **Jiumen Xiaochi**, see ❷, a collection of traditional Beijing snack stalls re-created in a large courtyard which has a doorway guarded by white stone lions and large red lanterns.

XIHAI

Heading further north brings you to **Xihai** ❹ (West Lake), the only one of the lakes to have escaped gentrification. The willows hang lazily over the water, shading old fishermen, and locals stroll by the lake with their children – it is quite idyllic. Continuing to circle around the lakes, pass through Houhai Park, with the quietest boat-rental spot and well-known restaurant **Kong Yiji**, see ❸, offering a very pleasant rooftop dining area. Branching off down Liuyin Hutong is **Gong Wang Fu** (Palace of Prince Gong), the world's largest extant courtyard house and a popular destination for tour groups. Prince Gong, the brother of Emperor Xian Feng, founded the Qing dynasty's department of foreign relations in 1861. His home and its 5.7-hectare (14-acre) grounds,

including lush gardens, are now occupied by the China Conservatory of Music. The historic structures in the complex include Beijing's only preserved Qing-dynasty theatre.

QIANHAI

The most commercially developed part of Shichahai, **Qianhai** ❺ (Front Lake) is lined with bars, cafés and restaurants to draw in the passing crowds. Here, you will also encounter pedicabs offering *hutong* tours of the alleyways and sites around the lake. Expect to pay 180 yuan for 2.5 hours, though reports of overcharging are common. Simply getting lost in the alleyways on foot by striking out westwards is a great way to see the neighbourhood; alternatively, rent a bicycle from one of the many rental outlets around the lake. Or head east to try out **Great Leap Brewing**, see ❹. **Lotus Lane** (Hehua Shichang), at the south-western corner of Qianhai, has cafés and restaurants like **Wang Pangzi Donkey Burger**, see ❺, as well as some shops and high-end bars, or find Banchang Hutong for **Mao Mao Chong**, see ❻. There is nightly dancing and a variety of daytime activities, such as music and massages, around the arched entrance to the lane.

BEIHAI PARK

Cross Di'anmen Xidajie to the north entrance to **Beihai Park** ❻ (Beihai

Nine Dragon Screen

Gongyuan or North Lake Park; daily, summer 6.30am–10pm, winter 6.30am–10pm; charge). The area around the lake served as the imperial residence for every dynasty that had its capital in Beijing. After the end of the imperial era in 1925, Beihai Park was opened to the public, though **Zhongnanhai** (Central and Southern Lake), surrounded by a thick wall, remains the cloistered domain of the Chinese leadership as the site of the Politburo and State Council offices (closed to the public).

Beihai Park is great for strolls and for going out on the lake in a rented rowboat. On your boat cruise, first skirt the western shore to see the **Nine Dragon Screen** (Jiulongbi), one of three in the city, and said to offer protection from fire.

Miniature Western Heaven

About 200m/yds along the shore is **Miniature Western Heaven** ❼ (Xiaoxitian), built in 1770. A shrine to Guanyin, the Goddess of Mercy, it is a large square pagoda surrounded by a moat and four guard towers. Then, backtrack to the **Five Dragon Pavilion** (Wulongting), which is named after the zigzagging walkways linking them.

Jade Island

Just north of the Five Dragon Pavilion, board a ferry to **Jade Island** ❽ (Qiong Dao; every half hour, daily 9am–6pm). The boat stops in front of **Fangshan Restaurant**, see ❼, in the **Hall of Ripples** (Yilantang) complex. This is a potential

dinner (or lunch) destination, but explore the lovely imperial gardens first.

Turn right onto the covered walkway that leads to the **Pavilion of Shared Coolness** (Xiexiuting) and take the stone path up the hill. Climb to the **Plate for Gathering Dew** (Chenglupan), a bronze figure of a man holding a container over his head. Emperor Qianlong built this whimsical tribute to a Han-dynasty emperor who believed the dew was an elixir for immortality. On the north-west side of the hill is the **Building for Reading Old Inscriptions** (Yuegulou), which has stone tablets covered with 6th- and 7th-century calligraphy. On the summit is the **White Dagoba** ❾ (Baita), a 35m (115ft) shrine dating from 1651, built by Shunzhi, the first Qing-dynasty emperor to reign in Beijing, to commemorate the first visit to Beijing by a Dalai Lama.

Descend on the south side of the hill. Pass through the **Hall of Universal Peace** (Pu'andian), an official meeting room in the Qing dynasty. The last stop is the Lamaist **Temple of Eternal Peace** (Yong'ansi). When you emerge on the south side of the island, you come to an elegant marble bridge connecting the island to the shore. From here, you can see, or cross the bridge to visit, the **Round Town** (Tuancheng; daily 8am–4.30pm; charge). It was the administrative centre of 15th-century Dadu during the Yuan dynasty.

Leave Beihai Park by the south gate, where taxis await.

Boating on Behai

Tai chi in Behai Park

Food and drink

❶ HANI GEJIU

48 Zhonglouwan Hutong; tel: 6401 3318; daily 10am–10pm; $$

Tucked away behind the Bell Tower, this rustic restaurant serves good Yunnanese cuisine with a focus on the Hani minority. The fresh dishes and friendly service give the place a refreshing village feel.

❷ JIUMEN XIAOCHI

1 Xiaoyou Hutong, Houhai; tel: 6402 5858; daily 10am–10pm; $

Beijing's most famous traditional snacks are offered under this roof. Enjoy boiled tripe, soft beancurd, rice cakes, wontons and more.

❸ KONG YIJI

Shichahai Houhai Nanyan; tel: 6618 4917; daily 10am–2pm and 4–10.30pm; $$

This popular themed diner recreates the ancient flavours of Shaoxing, the southern hometown of famed writer Lu Xun. It is advisable to make a reservation.

❹ GREAT LEAP BREWING

6 Doujiao Hutong; tel:5717 1399; daily 2pm–midnight; $$

The original Great Leap location, located in a gorgeously renovated century-old walled courtyard perfect for whiling away an warm afternoon, cements its status as the iconic Beijing bar. The brewery kick-started a brewing craze with their idiosyncratic brews, which use local Chinese ingredients like Yunnanese honey or bitter Darshan tea. There's no kitchen but waiters will help you order in from nearby restaurants if you ask.

❺ WANG PANGZI DONKEY BURGER

80 Gulou Xidajie; tel: 8402 3077; daily 24 hours; $

Adventurous eaters should stop by Wang Pangzi (Fatty Wang's) for a taste of their signature donkey – yes, donkey – sandwiches. Dirt-cheap and very flavourful, the lean meat bears a similarity to corned beef, and is served in a flaky pastry crust. Service is brisk and sizes are small, making it perfect for a pit stop on a tour around the back lakes.

❻ MAO MAO CHONG

12 Banchang Hutong; tel: 6405 5718; daily 6pm–late; $$

This cosy hutong bar specializes in original spirit infusions and good-value cocktails. Their thin-crust pizzas are popular, though better treated as a light snack.

❼ FANGSHAN RESTAURANT

Inside the east gate of Beihai Park; tel: 6401 1889; daily 11am–2pm and 5–8pm; $$$

You'll be fed like an emperor in sumptuous rooms once inhabited by princes, with dishes often unrecognisable. The food can be more exciting to look at than to eat, and consists largely of delicacies more impressive for their rarity than their flavour. All the same, a meal here is an experience you won't repeat anywhere else.

Hall of Prayer for Good Harvests

TEMPLE OF HEAVEN

Early-morning exercise rituals in the Temple of Heaven Park, followed by an exploration of the temple complex, a stop at the Natural History Museum and shopping at Hongqiao Market.

> **DISTANCE:** 3.5km (2 miles)
> **TIME:** Half a day
> **START:** Temple of Heaven Park
> **END:** Hongqiao Market
> **POINTS TO NOTE:** The Tiantandongmen subway stop makes a convenient arrival point for the entrance via the east gate and along the Long Corridor. Alternatively, take a taxi to the south gate and approach the iconic Hall of Prayer for Good Harvests as the emperor did.

The Temple of Heaven complex was originally constructed between 1406 and 1429 under Emperor Yongle of the Ming dynasty. Every year at the time of the winter solstice, the emperor would come here in a magnificent procession lasting several days to honour his ancestors and to pray for a good harvest. There is an audio tour available at the gates.

TEMPLE OF HEAVEN PARK

Enclosed by a 5km (3-mile) -long wall, the **Temple of Heaven Park ❶** (Tian-

tan Gongyuan; park daily 6am–9pm, temple daily 8am–5.30pm; separate charges for park and temple) is the best place in Beijing to catch a glimpse of some traditional, and some not-so-traditional, forms of Chinese culture. Along the paths and among the trees, Beijing residents practise *qigong* to strengthen their internal systems through concentration and slow-motion exercises that stimulate breathing and circulation. Plan to arrive by 7am or earlier if you want to see early-morning enthusiasts of *qigong*, *taiji*, calligraphy, Peking opera and kite-flying. The **Long Corridor** (Changlang) on the east side of the Hall of Prayer for Good Harvests is the best spot for seeing activities of all kinds.

TEMPLE COMPLEX

The park is round in the north, representing Heaven, and square in the south, representing Earth. Walk through the park to get to the city's most elegant and most recognised structure, the **Hall of Prayer for Good Harvests** (Qiniandian).

Traditional drumming   *Hall of Abstinence*

Hall of Prayer for Good Harvests

This exquisite example of a Chinese wooden building was constructed without nails or cement. The round hall is 40m (130ft) high, its three levels covered with deep-blue tiles symbolising Heaven. The roof is supported by 28 pillars: the four central pillars represent the four seasons; the double ring of 12 pillars represents the 12 months and the traditional divisions of the Chinese day (each comprising two hours). Intricate carpentry created the dome high overhead; below are thrones where tablets commemorating ancestors were placed. Destroyed several times, the hall was rebuilt in 1890. The structure contains a plaque dedicated to the Emperor of Heaven – this was the closest the earthly emperor and his heavenly counterpart ever came to one another.

Imperial Vault of Heaven

Head south to the **Imperial Vault of Heaven** (Huangqiongyu), which is much smaller but has similar deep-blue roof tiles representing Heaven. Ancestral tablets were stored here until they were needed for prayer ceremonies. The imperial vault is now best known for its acoustics. If you stand on the first of the **Three Echo Stones** (Sanyinshi) in front of the entrance and clap, you will hear a single echo. Do the same on the second stone, you will hear a double echo; and on the third, a triple echo. Whisper into the **Echo Wall** that encloses the courtyard around the hall, and another person

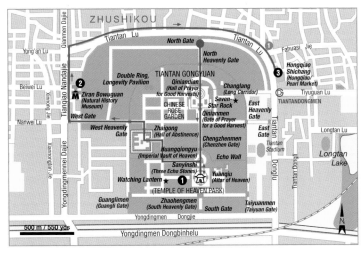

Pearls at Hongqiao Market

will be able to hear every word anywhere along the wall. Walk south to the **Altar of Heaven** (Yuanqiu), where three concentric terraces stand inside two enclosures – one square (symbolising Earth) and one round (Heaven). Animal sacrifices took place inside the square enclosure.

Hall of Abstinence

On the way to the west exit of the temple, you pass through the courtyard of the **Hall of Abstinence** (Zhaigong). The hall has a double moat spanned by a series of fine stone bridges, and its courtyard has a beautiful drum and bell tower. Twice a year, the emperor would spend a night of fasting and celibacy in the hall prior to the sacrificial rites the next morning. These rituals, which survived until 1914, go back 4,000 years.

NATURAL HISTORY MUSEUM

Leave by the west gate, just north of the Palace of Abstinence. Outside the gate, you come to the main north-south street, Tianqiao Nandajie, after about 100m/yds. Turn right and walk about 300m/yds to the **Natural History Museum ❷** (Ziran Bowuguan; daily 8.30am–5pm; charge). This is most famous for its large collection of dinosaur bones, gathered from other parts of China and Mongolia, as well as the endless numbers of dinosaur models. The exhibits on humanity's descent from apes are mildly interesting, while the human specimens are downright eerie.

HONGQIAO MARKET

A five-minute taxi ride will take you to the north-eastern corner of the park where the **Hongqiao Market ❸** (Hongqiao Shichang; daily 8.30am–7pm), or Pearl Market, stands across the street. This indoor market has everything from meat and spices to toys, clothes and antiques but it is known as the best place in Beijing to buy pearls. Be careful when making a purchase: fakes and low-quality specimen are rampant. Sellers may scrape the surface of a pearl to show it is not a painted bead – this is a good clue against the more flagrant fakes, but not a fail-safe test. If you are already here be sure to head to the fifth floor for the best available view of the Temple of Heaven Park.

Backtrack 300m/yds towards the north gate of the Temple of Heaven Park to arrive at **Old Beijing Noodle**, see ❶, the ideal spot for lunch.

Food and drink

❶ OLD BEIJING NOODLE

29 Chongwenmen Dajie; tel: 6705 6705; daily 11am–2.30pm and 5–9pm; $
This restaurant has revived the lively tradition of old-style Beijing fast food with hand-pulled noodles and other affordable dishes served in a rowdy atmosphere. *Zhajiang Mian*, noodles, served up with soybean paste and vegetables, are Beijing's most famous.

Wan Fung Art Gallery

TIANANMEN AND SANLITUN AT NIGHT

See a more tranquil side to the Tiananmen area, then trawl the buzzing Donghuamen Night Market, and onto Beijing's original bar street.

DISTANCE: 2km (1.5 miles)
TIME: Half a day, beginning from afternoon till late evening
START: Imperial City Art Gallery
END: Sanlitun
POINTS TO NOTE: Be sure to start early enough in the afternoon to catch the galleries before they close. Take a taxi or the subway to the Tian'anmen Dong stop to get to the Imperial City Art Gallery. This tour is mainly done on foot. From the city centre, take a taxi to Sanlitun.

Night-time sees a very different side to the Tiananmen area. By day, the Forbidden City and Tiananmen Square are tourist magnets; by night the outer wall of the Forbidden City is hauntingly peaceful. One reason could be the unspoken sense of taboo or superstition that many Beijingers still feel around the former residence of the emperors. Nearly a hundred years after the end of the empire, the old injunction against commoners entering the palace has yet to fade completely in the minds of Beijingers, and many will not visit at night.

ART GALLERIES

Begin your tour at the **Imperial City Art Gallery ❶** (Huangcheng Yishuguan; daily 10am–5.30pm), one of the city's newer museums, located in Changpuhe Park. The exhibits here are artefacts and artworks from the Forbidden City, including clothing and sumptuous articles of daily use. In addition, there is usually also a high-profile exhibition of art from abroad.

Across Nanchizi Dajie from the Imperial City Art Gallery is **Huangshicheng ❷**, the oldest-surviving imperial archival vault in the country. Built in 1536, it held national records, imperial genealogies and legal compendia during the Ming and Qing dynasties. It now houses two galleries of interest: the **Wan Fung Art Gallery** (Mon noon–6pm, Tue–Sun 10am–6pm) and the **New Art Centre** (daily 9am–5.30pm). Both galleries specialise in contemporary, though not necessarily modern, art by local Chinese ink artists.

Street food at Donghuamen Night Market

TIANANMEN SQUARE

After your tour of the galleries, leave Nanchizi Dajie and head to **Tiananmen Square ❸** for the flag-lowering ceremony, which is held at sunset, around 5.30pm in winter and 7.30pm in summer. The ceremony is one of the last few Soviet-style rituals China still practises. To encourage patriotism, it was beefed up with more soldiers and a taller flagpole. Hundreds gather each evening to watch the military drill and the flag-lowering, and thousands come on 1 May (International Workers' Day) and 1 October (China's National Day). But soon after the flag descends, quiet settles over the square. After the lights on the Monument to the People's Heroes and the Tiananmen Gate come on, the square seems a very different place.

Approaching the Forbidden City

Begin your walk by crossing under Dongchang'an Jie via the pedestrian tunnel. Walk through the Tiananmen Gate and follow the 600m/yd approach from the Tiananmen Gate to the Meridian Gate (Wumen), the entrance to the Forbidden City. When you reach the Meridian Gate, take a right and walk along the perimeter of the

Forbidden City, between its high wall and the moat.

DONGHUAMEN

Leave the Forbidden City via the side gate and take an immediate left. This road runs between the palace and the moat, so you won't get lost. After 50m/yds, it turns right, goes straight for another 400m/yds and turns left where there is another 50m/yd stretch. At this point you see the east gate of the Forbidden City on the left. Located here as well is **TRB Bites**, see ❶, one of the top fine-dining restaurants in the city. The road bends right and becomes **Donghuamen Night Market ❹** (Donghuamen Yeshichang),

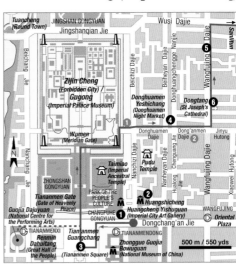

The bright lights of Sanlitun bar district

where you can find some of the most varied snacks and street food in town. Try a bowl of red-bean porridge or grilled quail if you are feeling peckish, or a stick of fried locusts if you dare.

If you need a more substantial meal, you are in luck, as you have just reached a strip of restaurants largely owned by, and catering to, overseas Chinese. There is good seafood and Cantonese restaurants on both sides of the street, such as the swanky **Hong Kong Food City**, see ②.

WANGFUJING STREET

After dinner, continue east to **Wangfujing Dajie** ❺, Beijing's premier shopping street (see page 34). Head north up on Wangfujing Dajie to **St Joseph's Cathedral** ❻ (Dongtang; see page 35). Also known as the East Cathedral and illuminated at night, it was originally built in the 17th century. It has been restored many times and is now spruced up as the district's main feature.

SANLITUN

To round off the evening, hop into a taxi to **Sanlitun**, a perennial favourite on Beijing's nightlife scene. Its 'Bar Street' runs along Sanlitun Lu, north of the Workers' Stadium, though the aggressive touts here mostly succeed only in pulling in tourists. Those in the know head straight to Nali Patio – a white, Mediterranean-style plaza packed with upmarket restaurants and bars – or

cross the street to Sanlitun South, a hidden-away area south of the intersection packed with international restaurants and bustling bars like ultra-cool Janes and Hooch (see page 113). Sanlitun Houjie, a rather grubby street that is slowly going upmarket, has two decent pubs (The Tree and First Floor), while there are some nice outdoor and rooftop spots north of Sanlitun Lu to explore.

Food and drink

❶ TRB BITES

95 Donghuamen Lu; tel 6401 6676; www.trb-bites.com; daily 11.30am–10.30pm; $$$

The sister establishment of fine dining Temple Restaurant Beijing, TRB Bites follows through on its more casual branding. Choose three, four or five modern European dishes to make up your meal (only desserts is fine!) while looking out at the serene Forbidden City moat.

❷ HONG KONG FOOD CITY

18 Dong'anmen Dajie; tel: 6525 7349; daily 11am–midnight; $$

One of Beijing's few options for authentic Cantonese dim sum. *Chashao bao* (steamed pork buns) and roast goose are the favourites. The atmosphere may be fancy, but this place is still suited for the kind of meals that dim sum is made for – long afternoons with family and friends, with round after round of tasty snacks.

An alleyway in Southern Beijing

DAZHALAN AND LIULICHANG

Walk through the old neighbourhood of Dazhalan with its warren of shops, into Liulichang, a restored section of the old city that is jam-packed with old shops selling curios and antiques, then onto the famous Ox Street Mosque.

> **DISTANCE:** 5km (3 miles)
> **TIME:** Half a day
> **START:** Qianmen
> **END:** Ox Street Mosque
> **POINTS TO NOTE:** Exploring the dirty, unreconstructed hutong of the Qianmen area is half the fun of a visit. Use common sense when judging the standard of hygiene of the food on offer.

The southern area of Beijing has long been the poorer side of town, ever since the Manchu invasion of 1644 relocated the local Han Chinese here, away from nobles and military officials who chose to reside in elegant homes further north. The streets deviate from the strict grid pattern of most of Beijing; the pavements are narrower and the drainage inferior. A massive development project centred on Qianmen Dajie in recent years has meant the beginning of the end for many of the old alleyways with their messy but characteristic way of life. The Muslim Quarter still offers a more authentic experience within easy reach of the city centre.

QIANMEN AREA

Arriving at Qianmen subway station, take the southern exit to emerge at the entrance to **Qianmen Dajie ❶**, with the glamorous façade of **Capital M**, see ❶, to greet you. This pedestrianised shopping street has been done up in traditional style and stretches into the distance with many smaller streets, often packed with tiny snack shops and food stalls, branching off to the east and west. High rents have driven many traditional businesses away from the Qianmen area since its makeover but the local government has been experimenting with subsidising the city's time-honoured brands operating here in hopes of keeping the 'old Beijing' theme alive.

Opened in 2011, the **Xianyukou Food Street** is mostly lined with traditional Beijing businesses. Enter through a gate marked by two giant red fish and sample wares such as stewed liver and red bean paste-filled rice cakes. There are also dumplings and steamed buns on sale for the less adventurous.

Market in Dazhalan   *Roadside chess on Xidamochang Jie*

DAZHALAN STREET

Dazhalan Jie ❷, a bustling *hutong* heading west of Qianmen Dajie boasts a 600-year heritage and is famous for its old shops. The name Dazhalan (often refered to as 'Dashilar' in Beijing dialect) literally means 'big stockades', and is an echo of Ming times when the streets were closed off at the evening curfew.

About 20m/yds along on the right is a building with extravagant wrought-iron gatework in green. This is **Hou Cheng Yi** (daily 9am–8.30pm), with a wide choice of fabrics on the second floor. Two doors down is **Ruifuxiang Silk and Cotton Fabric Store** (daily 9am–8pm), with a somewhat pretentious marble entrance. Ruifuxiang was built in 1893 by a Shandong businessman and catered to society's upper crust.

At No. 22 Dazhalan Xijie is **Zhang Yiyuan Tea Shop** (daily 8am–8pm), with bas-relief floral designs under its windows. More than a century old, Zhang Yiyuan stocks tea leaves. Next door at No. 24 is **Tongrentang Traditional Medicine Shop** (daily 8am–7.30pm), once responsible for keeping secret medicinal recipes for emperors. It has been here since 1669, and its pharmacists still weigh age-old herbal remedies with hand-held scales.

A little further down, at No. 36, is the grand entrance to **Daguanlou** (daily 9am–midnight), the oldest operating cinema in the world. Originally a teahouse that put on opera performances, the venue started to show foreign short films between acts in 1903.

YANGMEI ALLEYWAY

About 300m/yds further along Dazhalan Jie, you arrive at another junction. Turn right and then, another 30m/yds on, turn left. This is **Yangmei Hutong** ❸, a typical alleyway with children and old people in the street and the smells of cooking and communal toilets mingled together. Recent years have seen this dusty alley become a model of hutong development, with upmarket coffee shops, quirky restaurants and design stores. Most of the doors lead into *siheyuans*, courtyards with rooms facing inwards.

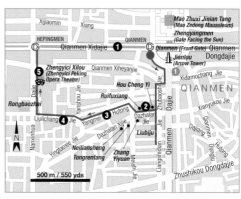

Curio shop in Liulichang

LIULICHANG STREET

After another 400m/yds, Yangmei Hutong takes a little jog to the right. There is an antiques shop on your left. Turn left onto **Liulichang Jie** ❹, packed with shops selling curios and antiques. This has been a shopping area for books and antiques for over 300 years.

During the Ming dynasty, Liulichang, which means 'glazed-tile factory', was one of the areas where tiles were made for imperial buildings. Later, it developed into a cultural centre for scholar-officials, who came here to stock up on calligraphy materials, books and seals. These days, Liulichang has reverted to its old function as a purveyor of paper and inks, patronised by serious calligraphers. Check out **Rongbaozhai** (daily 9am–5.30pm), a 17th-century shop at No. 19 Liulichang Xijie. It is famous for its range of watercolour paintings, calligraphy works, charcoal rubbings and painting materials.

ZHENGYICI PEKING OPERA THEATRE

Continue on to Nanxinhua Dajie and turn right. A few hundred metres north, before the Hepingmen subway stop, turn right onto Xiheyan Dajie. In the alleyway is the **Zhengyici Peking Opera Theatre** ❺ (Zhengyici Xilou; performances every evening; tel: 8315 1649). More than 330 years old, it is the only traditional theatre in the city to have its original, all-wood construction completely preserved.

TEMPLE OF THE SOURCE OF BUDDHIST DOCTRINE

A subway journey from Hepingmen to Caishikou subway station (change at Xuanwumen) takes you to Guanganmennei Dajie. Head east for 200m/yds then south along Xizhuan Hutong to find **The Temple of the Source of Buddhist Doctrine** ❻ (Fayuansi; Thur–Tue 8.30–11.30am and 1.30–3.30pm; charge). The maze of *hutong* can be rather confusing so you might consider taking a taxi here. This is one of the oldest-surviving Buddhist temples in Beijing, built in AD 645, and houses the Buddhist Academy. The academy trains novice monks, who are then despatched to monasteries across China. It has a library of

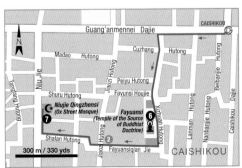

Chinese paint brushes

more than 100,000 precious texts and an exhibition of Buddhist sculptures, some dating from the Han dynasty. The large complex has six halls which are entered through Shanmen (Mountain Gate). In the first temple courtyard, two bronze lions guard the Hall of the Celestial Kings (Tianwangdian). Enthroned in the middle of the hall is a Milefo, a laughing, fat-bellied Buddha. The Hall of Heroes (Daxiongbaodian) contains a Buddha surrounded by 18 Luohan, the lowest rank in the Buddhist divine hierarchy. This is reached by leaving the first hall and crossing a garden with a bronze cauldron and stone steles. In the last hall is a reclining Buddha and a splendid Guanyin Bodhisattva with 1,000 arms. Stroll past the gardens on Fayuansi Qianhutong towards Niu Jie (Ox Street).

OX STREET MOSQUE

Built in AD 996, **Ox Street Mosque** ❼ (Niujie Qingzhensi; daily 8am–4pm; charge), has all the features of mosques found elsewhere in the world – a minaret, Arabic inscriptions and a prayer hall facing Mecca – but all in Chinese-style buildings. Islam arrived in China during the Tang dynasty via Arab merchants, and Muslims now live in all parts of the country.

This mosque is a gathering place for the city's Muslim community. Female visitors need not cover up their heads to enter, but shorts and short skirts are not allowed (the caretaker can lend you a pair of loose trousers). Non-Muslims cannot enter the prayer hall. Right behind the main entrance is a hexagonal building, the Tower for Observing the Moon (Wangyuelou). Every year, at the beginning and at the end of the fasting month of Ramadan, the imam climbs the tower to observe the waxing and waning of the moon and to determine the exact length of the period of fasting.

Hui shops and schools in the area around the mosque are signs of the community's unique Muslim background. Round the day off with dinner at **Da Shun Tang**, see ❷, where you have the chance to try some Muslim dishes.

Food and drink

❶ CAPITAL M

2 Qianmen Dajie; tel: 6702 2727; daily 11.30am–10.30pm; $$$
The sister restaurant to Shanghai's famous M on the Bund. The Qianmen location affords impressive terrace views across Tiananmen Square to match the glamorous interior and fine continental dining. Afternoon tea served from 2–5pm.

❷ DA SHUN TANG

5 Fayuansi Xili; tel: 010-6353 0644; daily 10.30am–9pm; $$
A popular choice of the local Hui community for its halal food that, typically, focuses on lamb. The stir-fried lamb and entrail soup are specialities.

Marble Boat on Kunming Lake

THE SUMMER PALACE

This route takes in the great landscaped gardens and lavish palaces built outside Beijing for the pleasure of the Empress Dowager Cixi in 1888. The tour is very popular, so expect crowds at the weekend.

DISTANCE: 2km (1.5 miles)
TIME: Half a day
START: The north gate
END: Sackler Gallery
POINTS TO NOTE: To get to the palace, take the subway to either Xiyuan or Beigongmen stations, or you can take a taxi. Though the basic layout can be traversed in half a day, the huge park can provide a much longer walk for those who want to see more of its sights.

The **Summer Palace** (Yiheyuan; daily, summer 6.30am–8.30pm, winter 7am–7pm; charge) was built in the late Qing dynasty to replace the nearby Old Summer Palace (Yuanmingyuan), which was destroyed by the European Eight Allied Armies in 1860 in the Second Opium War. In 1900, a large part of the palace was destroyed by Europeans during the Boxer Rebellion, when the anti-foreign rebels laid siege to foreigners in Beijing.

The notorious Empress Dowager Cixi fulfilled a wonderful but expensive dream in 1888 when she created this sprawling playground – the grounds cover more than 30 sq km (10 sq miles) – using 30 million taels of silver that was originally intended for a naval fleet. Cixi loved her new creation. She and her entourage effectively abandoned the Forbidden City and ruled China from here for 20 years until her death in 1908.

Arriving at Beigongmen subway station leads you into the park via Suzhou Street, created as a replica of a 19th-century canal-side shopping area in Suzhou, for Cixi and her court to enjoy the pleasures of shopping without having to mix among ordinary mortals.

Longevity Hill

Ascend from Suzhou Street into the square towers and stupas of the **Sumeru Temple** (Xumilingjing) and then down into the **Temple of the Sea of Wisdom** ❶ (Zhihuihai) at the top of Longevity Hill. Built in 1750, the temple is covered with countless Buddhas in the niches of its greenish-yellow ceramic facade. Many of the lower Buddhas were either smashed or beheaded by Red Guards during the

Hall of Benevolence opulence　　　　　　　　　*Temples of the Summer Palace*

Cultural Revolution. There are good views of the lake from this spot and a wonderful panoramic view of the whole palace further on at the massive octagonal **Pagoda of Buddhist Virtue** ❷ (Foxiangge), the highest point of the park. Connected to the pagoda by decorated corridors is the **Hall of Virtuous Light** (Dehuidian) and the **Hall of Dispelling Clouds** ❸ which comprises 21 rooms housing some valuable artefacts including the throne Cixi would sit upon to receive gifts on her birthday. Adjacent, on the west side, is one of the few buildings that survived the destruction of 1900 undamaged, the **Pavilion of Precious Clouds** ❹ (Bao-

yunge). In Cixi's day, Lamaist monks gathered here to pray on the 1st and 15th day of every lunar month. Its stepped roof makes it look like a wooden building yet was cast from bronze in 1750.

The Long Corridor

The **Long Corridor** ❺ (Changlang) is a magnificent example of a Chinese covered walkway. It runs parallel to the shore of Kunming Lake for 728 metres (796 yds). The ceilings and rafters are decorated with countless bird-and-flower motifs. At the end of the Long Corridor lies the famous **Marble Boat** ❻ (Qingyanfang), misleadingly named as it is

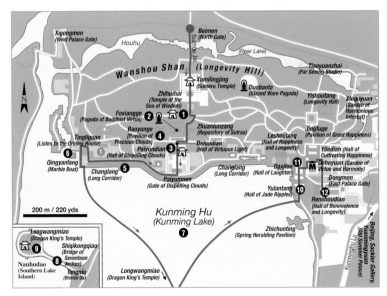

The Long Corridor

neither made of marble nor capable of floating. Make a stop at **Tingliguan** restaurant, see ❶, which is close by.

Boat tour

From the Marble Boat, it is possible to cross **Kunming Lake** ❼ (Kunming Hu) by 'dragon boat', landing either on Nanhudao (Southern Lake Island) or on the neighbouring mainland just south of the Hall of Jade Ripples (Yulantang). Close to the bridge leading to Nanhudao crouches the **Bronze Ox** (tongniu). Its task is to pacify the water spirits and to protect the surrounding land from floods. **The Bridge of Seventeen Arches** ❽ (Shiqikongqiao) crosses the water in a supremely grace-

ful curve, linking Nanhudao with the mainland. On the small island itself is the **Dragon King's Temple** ❾ (Longwangmiao) where Cixi would pray for rain in times of drought.

The eastern shore

The **Hall of Jade Ripples** ❿ is a courtyard building that served as Emperor Guangxu's bed chamber during his visits to the park and also his prison after Cixi supposedly put him under house arrest here for his recklessness at attempting to reform a crumbling dynasty by opening China to foreign ideas in 1898. Not far from the Hall of Jade Ripples, the refurbished **Hall of Laughter** ⓫ (Daxilou) was where Cixi and her court sat to view performances at an open-theatre called the Garden of Virtue and Harmony (Deheyuan). Today, Deheyuan serves as a theatre museum. In the lavish **Hall of Benevolence and Longevity** ⓬ (Renshoudian), with its opulent furnishings and objets d'art, Cixi held audiences with ministers and handled other business.

Old Summer Palace

The Old Summer Palace (Yuanmingyuan) is equally worth visiting. This sprawling complex was once the playground of Qing emperors. Utterly unlike its newer neighbour, it was distinguished from other imperial palaces by its unique architecture. It blended a variety of European styles into a dreamlike jumble that placed formal labyrinths next to Roman-style villas. The Old Summer Palace took the brunt of the invasion of the European Eight Allied Armies in 1860, and in subsequent decades was further dismantled by local residents. It has been left more or less in its original state of destruction, outfitted with signage as a reprimand to forgetful Westerners.

Food and drink

❶ TINGLIGUAN

Near the Marble Boat; tel: 6288 1955; www.tingliguan.com; daily 11am–2pm and 5–7pm; $$$

Tingliguan serves dishes that were popular at the imperial court. Fresh fish caught from Kunming Lake is a house speciality.

Child's play in Beijing

BEIJING FOR KIDS

Beijing's most famous attractions, such as the Forbidden City or the Great Wall, may not always appeal to younger travellers. But the city can also offer entertainment for children – and relief for their parents.

DISTANCE: 3.5km (2 miles)
TIME: Half a day
START: FunDazzle
END: Ritan Park
POINTS TO NOTE: Take a taxi to the south gate of the Workers' Stadium. You can either take a taxi or walk from the Workers' Stadium to Ritan Park. The walk ends at the south gate of Ritan Park, within walking distance of the Yong'anli subway stop.

Beijing has both good and bad points when it comes to travelling with children. On the one hand, the city can appear drab and unexciting, and it seems like there is nowhere that is safe from swerving taxis. On the other hand, Beijingers are enormously protective towards children. You will find that the average stranger will go out of his or her way to keep your little ones from danger (though you may get a scolding afterwards). Moreover, the city does conceal a number of pleasant locations that, once discovered, are perfect for keeping your children entertained.

FUNDAZZLE

Parents in Beijing know that for kids of younger ages, **FunDazzle** ❶ (Fandoule; east of the south gate of the Workers' Stadium; tel: 6506 9066; daily 9am–5.30pm; charge) provides endless entertainment, with arcade games, jungle gyms, ball rooms and more. Most younger kids are willing to stay all day.

BLUE ZOO

Not far to the west from FunDazzle is the **Blue Zoo** ❷ (Fuguo Haidi Shijie; inside the south gate of the Workers' Stadium; tel: 6591 3397; open 8am–6.30pm; charge), supposedly the largest aquarium of its kind in Beijing. The **Beijing Zoo** (137 Xizhimenwai Dajie; tel: 6831 4411; daily 7.30am–5pm) in western Beijing also has an aquarium; however, the popularity of the zoo ensures that on any day nice enough to visit, a substantial percentage of the city will be there ahead of you. The Blue Zoo promises a far less harrowing experience.

The Blue Zoo's submerged underwater tunnel

The Blue Zoo aquarium sports a 3.5 million-litre tank of artificial sea water that forms a walk-through aquarium supporting a complete mini-ecosystem of sea creatures. Several smaller tanks hold a variety of other sea life, including sharks. Shark feeding shows are put on twice daily and snorkelling and scuba lessons can be taken when instructors are available. In fact, all sorts of underwater activities are popular here, even an underwater marriage or two.

RITAN PARK

From Gongren Tiyuchang Nanlu, walk south for 20 minutes, or take a taxi if time is short. South of Chaoyangmenwai Dajie is **Ritan Park ❸** (Ritan Gongyuan; daily 6am–9pm; free). Originally built in 1530, Ritan, the Altar of the Sun, was one of a set of eight altars, including Ditan, Yuetan, Shejitan and Tiantan (dedicated to the earth, moon, crops and heaven, respectively), which emperors would visit on set dates to make offerings to the powers of the cosmos. Ritan was used on the spring equinox, when emperors observed a ritual of changing clothes at the Dressing Hall, and sacrifices were brought from the Divine Depot and the Divine Kitchen to the Slaughter Pavilion.

Ritan Park, one of the oldest parks in the city, is also one of the most peaceful and pleasant. Its northern half is taken up by historical buildings and a few small museums and monuments. The atmosphere is tranquil, and made more

so by the elderly people who come here to sing, exercise and fly kites.

Young children will like the southern end of the park more. There is a small amusement park with merry-go-rounds and other rides, as well as a small monorail, for which per-entry tickets can be purchased. A large fish pond is kept stocked with carp and other edible fish, and fishing poles can be rented by the half-hour. Another small lake is equipped with small remote-controlled boats (or ice-sleds when it is frozen over in winter), which are the only real disturbance to the peace. And if you bring your young ones to Ritan

The lakeside pavilion in Ritan Park

Park on a nice weekend, there will be numerous other local children, who will be happy to welcome them into their games.

There are no lack of dining options in this part of town, though since this is an embassy district there is a higher-than-average concentration of Western options. If you're feeling up for some local cuisine, make a beeline to the park's north entrance to **Xiao Wang Fu**, see ❶, a gentle introduction into Chinese cooking with nothing that should scare off picky eaters. If your children are fussy or you simply fancy something simple, consider burgers and milkshakes at **Grandma's Kitchen**, see ❷, further south or reliable pizza and pasta at **Annie's** Italian restaurant, see ❸, within the Ritan Highlife development opposite the north gate.

Imported Western snacks suitable for a picnic can be found at **Jenny Lou's**, see ❹. The area is in fact full of restaurants – stroll down Guanghua Lu or Ritan Lu further south for more choices.

Lastly, if your child is experiencing any health problem, this is also the place to come to. The **Bayley and Jackson Medical Centre** (tel: 010-8562 9998; www.bjhealthcare.com) on Ritan Donglu has a paediatrics centre, with doctors who are fluent in English.

Food and Drink

❶ XIAO WANG FU
North gate of Ritan Park; tel: 8561 9585; daily 11am–2pm, 5.30–10pm daily; $$
A popular foreigner-friendly introduction to Chinese cuisine, with accessible classic Chinese dishes served just inside the park. Ask for a seat on the second-floor rooftop on a nice day.

❷ GRANDMA'S KITCHEN
11 Xiushui Nanjie; tel: 6503 2893; daily 9am–10pm; $$
When it has been a long slog through China and the kids have gone on hunger strike, Grandma's Kitchen may be your only recourse. American-style burgers, thick shakes and skillet scrambles, served in a down-home atmosphere just on the far side of kitsch, ought to restore the spirits of the most recalcitrant little troopers.

❸ ANNIE'S
Unit 2, Ritan High Life, 39 Shenlu Jie; tel: 8569 3031; daily 11am–11pm; $$
Simple, Italian-American food including pizza and a family friendly atmosphere that even extends to special play areas for the little ones.

❹ JENNY LOU'S
4 Ritan Beilu; tel: 8563 0626; daily 8am–midnight; $–$$
One of a chain of import supermarkets, Jenny Lou's caters to foreigners, Westerners in particular, who are looking for a taste of home. Sliced bread, cold cuts, sausage rolls, cakes, fruit juices and canned drinks are all available.

OLD AND NEW BEIJING

Beijing is one of the oldest – and fastest-changing – capitals in the world. This route moves from the Central Business District, the city's most modern sector, to some of its oldest neighbourhoods, revealing the ways in which the past and the future intermesh.

DISTANCE: 7.5km (5.5 miles)
TIME: A full day
START: World Trade Centre
END: New Poly Plaza
POINTS TO NOTE: Start from the Guomao subway stop. After exploring the CBD, either walk to Jinbao Jie, or take the subway to the Jianguomen stop, and head north from there to Dongsi Shitiao.

The heart of Beijing's new downtown is the **World Trade Centre ❶**, also known as Guomao. This part of town was still farmland when Guomao was built in the late 1980s, but a combination of market forces and energetic city planning has turned this area into the economic heart of the modern capital. The CBD (Central Business District) now occupies an area of roughly 4 sq km (1.5 sq miles), dominated by innovative works of architecture.

NEW BUSINESS DISTRICT

The jewel in the crown of the CBD is the **China Central Television Station**
Tower ❷ (Zhongyang Dianshitai; CCTV), just across Dongsanhuan Lu from Guomao. The tower was conceived by international superstar architect Rem Koolhaas, and built for a rumoured 850 million euros. It was designed with an industrial workflow in mind – one 'leg' is devoted to broadcasting, the other to research and planning, and the joining section at the top houses management.

Beginning from the CCTV Tower, wander at will in the CBD. The **China World Trade Centre Tower III** is Beijing's tallest building at 330m (1,083ft) a number you can appreciate from the 80th floor at **Atmosphere Bar**, see ❶. South of the World Trade Centre, the uniform, boxlike home/office complex **Jianwai SOHO** is hard to miss. Built by Chinese 'starchitect' real estate developer Pan Shiyi, the iconic design will doubtlessly shape the blueprint of the future CBD.

SILK MARKET

If the weather is nice and it is early, stroll down Guanghua Lu from the CBD to Erhuan Lu (Second Ring Road). This

A view of Beijing's CBD

leafy neighbourhood is one of Beijing's two embassy districts, and is surprisingly peaceful despite its location in the middle of town. On your way, pop into the **Silk Market ❸** (Xiushui Shichang), home to brand-name counterfeit goods. You can also choose to take the subway from Yong'anli to Jianguomen.

ANCIENT OBSERVATORY

At the junction of Jianguomennei and the Second Ring Road is the **Ancient Observatory** (Gu Guangxiangtai) **❹**.

Originally constructed in 1279 north of its present-day site, the observatory that you see today was built in the mid-15th century and sits atop a watchtower that was once part of the city walls. It served both the Ming and Qing dynasties in making predications based on astrology, as well as helping navigators who were about to go to sea. It remains an evocative reminder of the era in which Jesuit priests advised Chinese emperors, and reading the stars was of crucial importance to governance.

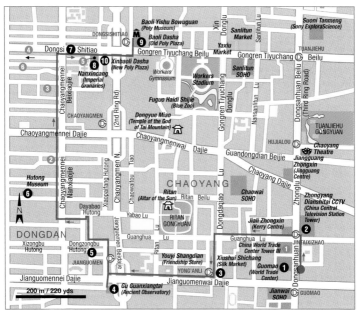

The Silk Market

ZONGBU HUTONG

Not far from the Jianguomen subway stop is **Dongzongbu Hutong** ❺, leading west from Jianguomen Beidajie. The three sections of **Zongbu Hutong** are some of the oldest-surviving streets in Beijing, dating back at least 600 years. Foreign ambassadors lived here during the invasion of the European Eight Allied Armies in the late 19th century, and negotiations between the Communists, Nationalists and Americans during China's civil war also took place here.

From here, you can continue on to **Xizongbu Hutong** and explore the old buildings; otherwise, find the entrance to **Beizongbu Hutong** and head north. At the northern end of the alleyway, on the right, is the **former residence of Liang Sicheng**. During the 1920s and 1930s, the intellectual and his wife Lin Huiyin held a cultural salon here, which was attended by many of the greatest artists and reform-minded thinkers of the day.

Go further west to Chaoyangmen Nanxiaojie, cross the street to the west side, and head north from there. Here are old, untouched neighbourhoods, with tree-shaded lanes winding back among the courtyards, filled with bicycles and people.

If it is time for lunch, there is plenty of simple street food in this area, plus a wealth of restaurants. One excellent choice is **Qin Tang Fu**, see ❷, serving authentic Shaanxi noodles. Otherwise, proceed further past Chaoyangmennei Dajie to find even more choices.

Shijia Hutong Museum

About halfway up Chaoyangmen Nanxiaojie, turn west onto Shijia Hutong, one of the few hutongs that have been protected in its entirety. It's the site of the **Shijia Hutong Museum** ❻ (Shijia Hutong Bowuguan; 24 Shijia Hutong; 9.30am–noon, 2–4pm Tue–Sun; free), the first (and so far only) museum specifically established to remember the vanishing hutong way of life. The compound was the residence of two notable Chinese authors, Chen Xiying and Ling Shuhua, and is unique in that the doors face north – customarily homes keep the entrance facing south to keep out frigid northern winds. Exhibits are mostly bilingual, and elaborate on the customs and lifestyle of hutong residents: one exhibition recreates hutong rooms of previous decades, and another plays the recorded sounds of street peddlars, knife sharpeners and signalling bells taken from a Beijing of long ago.

DONGSI SHITIAO

Return to the north-south route. The alleyways running off Chaoyangmen Nanxiaojie all have names based on their historical usage; those further north are known as **Dongsi Shitiao** (Ten Alleys of Dongsi) and are called by their numbers. These names have remained

View of hutong roofs

the same since the Ming dynasty, except for a brief period during the Cultural Revolution when they were known as the '18 Alleys of Red Sun Street'.

Further north in Dongsi Liutiao (Alley Six) is the Xinjiang restaurant **Crescent Moon** (Wanwan Yueliang), see ③. If you're in the mood for more than a simple dinner later tonight, make a reservation at the **Red Capital Club**, see ④, well in advance. Alternatively, pop around Dongsi Batiao (Alley Eight) for a pint at the **Slow Boat Brewery Taproom**, see ⑤, one of Beijing's most popular gastropubs.

NANXINCANG

Turn right onto the street of **Dongsi Shitiao** ❼ (sometimes called Ping'an Dajie) and head towards Erhuan Lu (Chaoyangmen Beidajie/Chaoyangmen Nandajie). Before you reach Dongsi Shitiao Bridge, you will see a cluster of old-looking buildings on the south side of the street. During the Ming and Qing dynasties, these were the *huang-jia liangcang* – imperial granaries that stored food for emperors and their immediate families, ensuring that famine would never harm royalty. These old buildings have been remodelled and opened for limited use, and are now known as **Nanxincang** ❽. Though it had made many preservationists anxious, the reuse of the imperial granaries is now generally seen as a success. Strict rules governing the treatment of

the old buildings were put in place by experts (not officials) and, more surprisingly, enforced. This little area has since become a ritzy nightlife district. Three granary buildings are given over to the **Xin Beijing Art Gallery**; others house fancy restaurants, bars and clubs. An excellent dinner option here is **Dadong Peking Duck Restaurant**, see ⑥.

POLY PLAZAS

Situated kitty-corner from each other, across Dongsi Shitiao Bridge, are the old and new Poly plazas. In some ways, they stand for the great leap that Beijing's architecture has made in the past 20 years. The **Old Poly Plaza** ❾ (Baoli Dasha) is painted a drab yellow colour and houses the Poly Theatre. The **New Poly Plaza** ❿ (Xinbaoli Dasha), built by the US architectural firm SOM, is monumental without being overbearing, composed of an interesting combination of glass curtain walls and subtly coloured metal plating.

Poly Museum

The ninth floor is home to the **Poly Museum** (Baoli Yishu Bowuguan; tel: 6500 1188; Mon–Sat 9.30am–4.30pm; charge). Only a small part of the Poly Group's collection is on view, but every piece is a treasure. The main room features Buddha statues dating back to the Tang dynasty, and the exhibition design is masterful – the room hushed, each statue lit with a spot-

Fresh produce in Dongsi Shitiao

light, the air of antiquity palpable. Further on are a few bronze heads of the twelve animals of the Chinese zodiac (*shengxiao*), which were looted from the Old Summer Palace (Yuanmingyuan).

Food and drink

① ATMOSPHERE BAR

80th Floor, China World Trade Centre Tower III; tel: 6505 2299; $$$
The views from Beijing's tallest building are, unsurprisingly, impressive. Part of the Shangri-la Hotel, this lounge bar does in fact manage a decent atmosphere. Expensive but excellent cocktails and Japanese whiskies pad out the drinks menu.

② QIN TANG FU

69 Chaoyangmen Nanxiaojie; tel: 6559 8135; daily 11am–2pm and 5–10pm; $
Saozimian (sister-in-law's noodles) is the thing to get, or branch out for spicy mutton dumplings and pork sandwiches. Try a mug of the sweet white *choujiu* – a mild rice-based alcoholic drink – or sour plum juice. The dolls, paper-cut wall hangings, and knee-high tables are all typical of Shaanxi culture.

③ CRESCENT MOON

16 Dongsi Liutiao (Alley Six), about 100m/yds in from Chaoyangmen Beixiaojie; tel: 6400 5281; daily 10am–11.30pm; $
This is a few notches more authentic than most Xinjiang restaurants in Beijing. The food, such as mutton skewers (*yangrou chuan'r*) and 'big-plate chicken' (*da pan'r ji*), comes in Xinjiang-sized portions.

④ RED CAPITAL CLUB

66 Dongsi Jiutiao (Alley Nine); tel: 8401 6152; www.redcapitalclub.com.cn; daily 6pm–midnight; $$$
Ostensibly for the 'new red capitalists', this trades on its Mao-era memorabilia and atmosphere, offering a slice of privileged life as China's top leaders might have lived it. Thus you can enjoy plush surroundings, Red Flag limos and an impressive cigar selection.

⑤ SLOW BOAT BREWERY TAPROOM

56 Dongsi Batiao; tel: 6538 5537; Mon–Thu 5pm–midnight, Fri 5pm–1am, Sat 2pm–1am, Sun 11.30am–10pm; $
Slow Boat offers a great variety of creative American-style microbrews from IPAs to vanilla stouts. The pub fare of burgers, spicy fries and sausages is an excellent stomach liner if you're hanging around for a few pints.

⑥ DADONG PEKING DUCK

G/F, Nanxincang Office Towers; tel: 5169 0329; daily 11am–10pm; $$$
One of the best places in town for Peking duck. All Dadong chain restaurants are appallingly popular, so make a reservation at least a day in advance. Dadong is also known for duck dishes such as duck liver pate and duck soups.

The National Stadium

THE OLYMPIC PARK

The city planners went to great lengths to beautify the areas around the awe-inspiring facilities for the 2008 Olympics. This route brings you to the Olympic sights and Beijing's enormous forest park, the best way to escape the crowds, plus an ancient city wall and the Chinese Ethnic Culture Park.

> **DISTANCE:** 4.5km (2.75 miles)
> **TIME:** Half a day, or a full day if you linger in the forest park
> **START:** Tucheng Park
> **END:** Olympic Forest Park
> **POINTS TO NOTE:** Take the subway to the Beitucheng subway stop. Check ahead in case any special events are taking place at the Olympic stadiums.

The 4.8km (3-mile) long- **Tucheng Park** ❶ (Tucheng Gongyuan), your first stop, was once part of the city wall of Dadu, the capital of the Yuan dynasty. The wall was originally made of earth (*tucheng* means 'earthen wall'); only a few shapeless mounds remain, but the city moat, called Little Moon River (*Xiaoyuehe*), still exists.

ETHNIC CULTURE PARK

The **Chinese Ethnic Culture Park** ❷ (Minzuyuan; 1 Minzuyuan Lu; tel: 6206 3647; daily 8.30am–6pm; charge) showcases the various architectural and living styles of the 56 ethnic groups of China,

including the majority Han. While many minority groups are diverse enough to be split into two or even three, the categori-

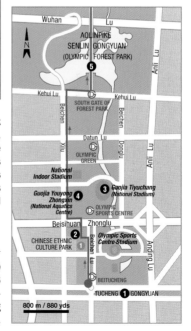

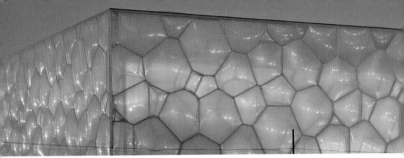

Distinctive design on the National Aquatics Centre

sation was established during the early days of the People's Republic and is politically non-negotiable. Typical dwellings of various ethnic minorities – from the Tibetans' inward-sloping forts to the slate-piled houses of the Bouyei – have been transported here from their native areas. Members of the various ethnicities have also been hired to represent their people in traditional dress. Though the minorities are each given a display that details their particular crafts, customs and beliefs, the emphasis always returns to cultural shows with singing and dancing, even if these activities do not figure much in some cultures. Be warned: the shows can be condescending and tacky.

Between the northern and southern sections of the park are a few restaurants serving ethnic food. Among them, **Caixianggen**, see ❶, serves authentic Hunanese food.

Food and drink

❶ CAIXIANGGEN

8 Minzuyuan Lu; tel: 6680 4025; daily 11am–2pm and 5pm till late; $$
Hunan is Chairman Mao's place of birth, and most Hunanese restaurants advertise themselves as serving 'Mao food'. Not Caixianggen, which forgoes some of the spicier, oilier dishes beloved by Mao in favour of greater variety. Try the radish and beef stew, bacon and bamboo root, and donkey meat, which is surprisingly tender.

OLYMPIC FACILITIES

Along with the chance to host the 2008 Olympics Games, Beijing also won a chance to give itself a complete makeover with some world-class architecture.

Head north from the Ethnic Culture Park and you come to the 3.5 billion-yuan **National Stadium** ❸ (Guojia Tiyuchang), designed by the Swiss firm Herzog & de Meuron. The 'Bird's Nest', as many Beijingers call it, has girders that function as both structure and façade. It's also open to tourists, and is one of Beijing's top attractions.

The **National Aquatics Centre** ❹ (Guojia Youyong Zhongxin; www.watercube.com; daily 9am–7pm; charge) was inspired by two Irish physicists' work on the structure of soap bubbles and has the local nickname of 'Water Cube'. Its walls are made of steel girders draped with a teflon-like material, which is inflated with pumps. The transparent walls trap energy from sunlight, providing a natural source of heating for the pools. The centre houses a water park and fitness facilities.

Olympic Forest Park

The **Olympic Forest Park** ❺ (Aolinpike Senlin Gongyuan), north of the sports facilities, is the city's largest green space. The 12.25 sq km (5 sq mile) park is a carefully constructed expanse of woods, lakes and meandering pathways with a bird reserve in the northern section and a garden to the south. The central Main Lake can be explored by rented pedalo.

Signage at the entrance to 798 Art District

MODERN ART

Since the turn of the century, Beijing's modern art scene has seen not only a vast proliferation of artists, but also widespread recognition from international art circles. This new renown has transformed Chinese art markets and also Beijing's art-viewing experience.

DISTANCE: 2km (1.25 miles)
TIME: A full day
START: 798 Art District
END: Caochangdi
POINTS TO NOTE: A taxi is more or less the only option here. Taxi drivers are becoming more aware of the 798 Art District, but you may have to direct your driver to Dashanzi Huandao and then north from there on to 798 on Jiuxianqiao Beilu. It is possible to walk from 798 to Caochangdi (half an hour), but it's far more pleasant to take a taxi. Note that most 798 Art District galleries are closed on Mondays.

Luckily for art enthusiasts, the vast majority of Beijing's modern art is concentrated in one area of town. The neighbourhood, called **Dashanzi**, is an old military factory district, a remnant of the early days of the PRC. The factories and warehouses here have partially been converted into artists' studios and galleries, while heavy machinery is still chugging right next to the exhibitions.

The first artists arrived here in 2001–2, including the designer Huang Rui, who is in some ways the artists' patron saint. In 2002, the inaugural art show was held, and artists flocked here to establish studios. At that time, the rent was as low as 0.1 yuan per square metre per day. By 2004, however, rental had gone up considerably, and in recent years artists' studios have largely been taken over by internationally funded galleries and fancy eateries.

798 ART DISTRICT

This tour begins at the 798 Art District. In the early days of the PRC, the country received a great deal of technical assistance from abroad, particularly from the Soviet Union. When the factories were built, in the early 1950s, they were numbered, rather than named. Although the art district has expanded to include the 781 area to the north, the name 798 has remained. That area (originally known as Factory 718) was the first major project undertaken with the help of the East Germans,

The gallery at 798 Space

instead of the Soviets. The Germans originally intended to design the buildings with local characteristics, but the Chinese, wanting to ensure success, told them to build as they did at home in Germany. The result is the unique Bauhaus look, best exemplified by the main 798 Space building. The windows face north (counter to Chinese tradition) because the northern light is indirect, casting fewer distracting shadows on the machinery. Coincidentally, the same principal makes for excellent art-viewing conditions

There is essentially a square kilometre of space here in which to wander freely. As you enter through the front gate, check out the large red map on the right-hand side, which will help you locate the galleries. There is another map on the main road further in. Public toilets are available here, but they are not always sanitary; it might be easier to visit one in a café or restaurant.

Otherwise, there is art of one sort or another to be found in the countless galleries and venues in 798 – the area can easily provide a weekend's worth of sights. The following are some of the better-known venues:

798 Space ❶ (tel: 6437 6248; www.798space.com; daily 10.30am–7.30pm) is one of the main venues in 798 for large-scale international exhibitions and the first space set up by Huang Rui and photographer Xu Yong, in 2002. It also hosts fashion shows and the annual Dashanzi International Art Festival.

Ullens Centre for Contemporary Art ❷ (tel: 8459 9269; www.ucca.org.cn; daily 10am–6pm) is a multi-million dollar not-for-profit exhibition space that sets itself apart by hosting impressive exhibitions and allowing visitors to take

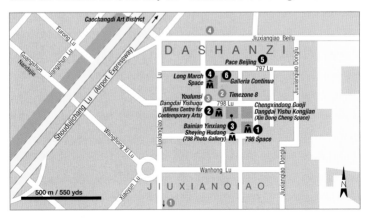

798 Photo Gallery   *Visiting an exhibition*

photographs. The museum also has an attached store selling designer clothes, art literature and original pieces from Chinese artists.

798 Photo Gallery ❸ (tel: 6438 1784; www.798photogallery.cn; daily 10am–6pm) consistently shows some of the best and most provocative photography in the 798 Art District.

Long March Space ❹ (tel: 6438 7107; www.longmarchspace.com; daily 11am–7pm) is one of the most active galleries in the area, Long March's success is mostly due to the curatorial vision of Lu Jie, who is one of the most internationally involved artist-curators in 798. He has arranged travelling art exhibitions in China and residencies for foreign artists.

Pace Beijing ❺ (tel: 5978 9781; www.pacegallery.com/beijing; Tue–Sat 10am–6pm) is the Beijing branch of the esteemed New York gallery intends to highlight both the best established

names and rising stars of the Chinese art scene, as well as the occasional international artist megastar.

Almost all of the exhibitions in **Galleria Continua ❻** (tel: 5978 9505; www.galleriacontinua.com; Tue–Sun 10am–6pm) are conceived and built specifically for the gallery space, resulting in some of the most immersive and extraordinary shows in Beijing.

For lunch or light refreshments, try **AT Café**, see ❶, for trendy fusion fare, or the **Timezone 8 Café**, see ❷, for something simpler. **Liangshi**, see ❸, and **Najia Xiaoguan**, see ❹, offer other good alternatives.

CAOCHANGDI

If the 798 Art District is too commercial for your artistic sensibilities there is also **Caochangdi**, a smaller art area not too far to the north. This satellite district came into being thanks to Ai Weiwei, one of the greatest and most controversial figures of Beijing's art scene. The son of a famous poet named Ai Qing, Ai Weiwei was a member of The Stars, one of the earliest art movements formed following the end of the Cultural Revolution. His China Art Archives and Warehouse (CAAW) opened in Caochangdi in 2000, when the area was just farmland, but it has since attracted enough satellite venues to join it, making Caochangdi a district in its own right.

Caochangdi is not an easy area to negotiate. Walking here from 798 is

Chinese contemporary art at China Art Archives and Warehouse

possible, although not too pleasant – the walk is mostly along a highway. Taxi drivers may know of Caochangdi, but it is better to call a gallery and have the staff give directions to the driver.

China Art Archives and Warehouse ❻ (tel: 8456 5152; www.archivesandwarehouse.com; Wed–Sun 2–6pm) is the original Caochangdi venue and has hosted many ground-breaking exhibitions, mostly featuring Ai Weiwei's friends – meaning some of the top experimental artists in China.

Platform China ❼ (tel: 6432 0169; www.platformchina.org; Tue–Sun 11am–6pm) is as much a communications and art exchange organisation as it is a gallery. The gallery's focus is cutting-edge works by Chinese artists, including video and new media.

Three Shadows Photography Art Centre ❽ (tel: 6432 2663; www.three shadows.cn; Tue–Sun 10am–6pm) is an impressive courtyard gallery, designed by Ai Weiwei, and the first centre of contemporary photography in China.

Food and drink

❶ AT CAFÉ
4 Jiuxianqiao Lu; tel: 6438 7264; daily 10am–midnight; $$
This hip little eatery offers a small menu of pasta dishes, pastries and simple Chinese fare, along with a modest selection of wines and cocktails. With the same 'industrial chic' décor that characterises all of 798, it is a great spot to catch glimpses of famous artists.

❷ TIMEZONE 8 BAR AND RESTAURANT
4 Jiuxianqiao Lu; tel: 8456 0336; daily 8.30am–9pm; $
American Robert Bernell was the first foreigner to move in 798 all the way back in 2001 and this is an ideal pit stop for a meal in between gallery-hopping. There's also a good selection of imported brews and prime outdoor seating for people-watching. An unremarkable sushi bar is in the back.

❸ LIANGSHI
East of the Ullens Center of Contemporary Art; tel: 5762 6415; 10am–midnight daily; $
A restaurant just as artistic as the nearby galleries, Liangshi sports an eye-popping interior design of birdcages, chains and spotlights. If you can peel your eyes away from the decor, the restaurant offers light Cantonese fare and coffee.

❹ NAJIA XIAOGUAN
2 Jiuxianqiao North Road; tel: 5978 9333; daily 11am–9.30pm; $$
Located just outside the 798 district, this atmospheric restaurant recreates the hearty, elaborate dishes of the former Manchu nobility with the requisite aristocratic touch. Add in costumed waiters, birds that chirp 'ni hao' and a recreated imperial courtyard and you're a world away from the factories outside.

Temple of the Azure Clouds

FRAGRANT HILLS PARK

The temples and pavilions dotted around the Fragrant Hills Park, located north-west of the city, are a popular hiking destination and offer excellent views of the city on clear days.

> **DISTANCE:** 3km (1.5 miles)
> **TIME:** Half a day
> **START:** Temple of the Azure Clouds
> **END:** Beijing Botanical Gardens
> **POINTS TO NOTE:** This walk involves some hilly, though not difficult, terrain, so wear appropriate footwear and get an early start. If the weather permits, this is a good opportunity for a picnic lunch. There is also an option for a boat tour at the Summer Palace. From the city centre, take a taxi (around 50 yuan) or a bus (No. 714, 318, 331 or 904). Expect the journey to take an hour or more.

The **Fragrant Hills Park** (Xiangshan Gongyuan; daily, summer 6am–7pm, winter 6am–6pm; charge) was a favourite hunting retreat of emperors from the 12th to 18th centuries. A number of emperors made their mark here by building pagodas and temples. At the height of its popularity, during the Qing emperor Qianlong's reign, the walled park was filled with exotic deer. Mao Zedong lived here briefly in 1949, at Shuangqing Villa, before he moved to Zhongnanhai next to the Forbidden City. Much of the Fragrant Hills Park fell into decay or was destroyed by European armies between 1860 and 1900, but it has since been restored and is now one of the most popular destinations for day trippers from Beijing, particularly in the autumn to see the vibrantly coloured foliage. The mountainside is riddled with small paths and forgotten temples. If you're not in a hurry, exploration is guaranteed to be rewarding.

TEMPLE OF THE AZURE CLOUDS

The park's ticket office is just left of the main entrance. Once inside, follow the stone path that veers right and buy another ticket to visit the **Temple of the Azure Clouds ❶** (Biyunsi; daily 8am–5pm; charge). A temple was first built here in 1330 and later generations added new buildings, especially during the Qing dynasty. The first hall contains two huge celestial guardians, and the second has a statue of the Maitreya Buddha, all from the Ming dynasty.

Stone carving at the Diamond Throne Pagoda

The innermost hall is the **Sun Yat-sen Memorial Hall** (Sun Zhongshan Jiniantang), in memory of the leader of the Nationalist movement that overthrew the Qing dynasty. To the right of his statue is a crystal coffin, a rather macabre gift from the Soviet Union.

One of the temple's more unusual treasures is the Indian-style 35m (115ft) **Diamond Throne Pagoda** at the rear of the complex. On the first level is a sanctuary with carved monster heads. This held Sun Yat-sen's body from 1925 to 1929 before it was moved to Nanjing. Climb up the inner stairs to the top terrace, with its central tower surrounded by six small pagodas covered in carved bodhisattvas (enlightened beings).

After descending and passing the Sun Yat-sen Memorial Hall, on your right is the impressive **Hall of 500 Luohan** (500 Luohantang). Enter through the side gate in the lower terrace of this courtyard.

INCENSE BURNER PEAK

Walk down the hill from the temple the same way you came but turn right into Fragrant Hills Park proper just before you reach the exit. Another name for Fragrant Hills is **Incense Burner Peak ❷** (Xianglufeng), a description of its appearance when fog settles on the 557m (1,827ft) high summit. About 50m/yds along the path on the right is the ticket office for the cable car (daily 8.30am–5pm),

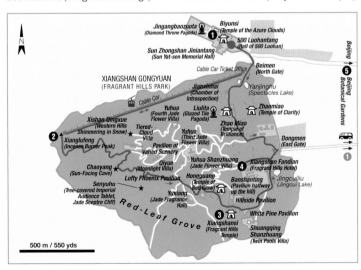

Spectacles Lake | *Entrance to the Temple of Clarity*

which substitutes a 15-minute ride for an hour's steep climb. On the right is the Diamond Throne Pagoda; to the left is **Spectacles Lake** (Yanjinghu), named for its resemblance to a pair of spectacles.

After admiring the view from the pavilion on the summit, you have two choices. You can take the cable car back to the bottom and head southwards, visiting Spectacles Lake and the **Temple of Clarity** (Zhaomiao). Pass the east gate (but do not exit), walk several hundred metres/yards along a leafy path that exits onto the main road leading to the Fragrant Hills Hotel. Turn right and walk 150m/yds to the hotel's main entrance.

If you have more energy, descend using the path down from the Incense Burner Peak, starting at the end of the pavilion furthest from the cable car terminus. The pleasant path zigzags through lush forest. On the way down – a 40-minute walk – take the right whenever the path forks. Halfway down, you pass an old hunting lodge, two more pavilions and the ruins of the **Fragrant Hills Temple** ❸ (Xiangshansi), in the clutches of some gnarled pines.

Fragrant Hills Hotel

Just beyond the temple, the path joins a road. Turn left and walk 100m/yds to the main gate of the **Fragrant Hills Hotel** ❹ (Xiangshan Fandian; tel: 010-6259 1166). This oasis of luxury, designed by Chinese-American architect I.M. Pei, embraces classical Chinese themes. In the expansive grounds, an elaborately crafted Chinese garden blends into the wooded surroundings. **Maimai Jie**, by the Fragrant Hills Hotel, is the main street leading to the front gate of the Fragrant Hills, and a carnival of street food and handicrafts. There is plenty to eat here including **Sculpting in Time**, see ❶.

Beijing Botanical Gardens

Less physically challenging than the mountain-top is the **Beijing Botanical Gardens** ❺ (Beijing Zhiwuyuan; daily, summer 6am–7pm, winter 7am–5pm; charge) at the foot of the hill about 2km (1.25 miles) from Biyunsi. Great expense has gone into making this a first-class garden, with extensive collections of flowers from around the world – this is the largest plant collection in China. Beautiful landscaping leads into hidden paths and glades on the skirts of the mountain. An enormous greenhouse (separate charge) houses tropical plants, ideal during Beijing's cold, dry and dusty winters.

Food and drink

❶ **SCULPTING IN TIME**
50 Maimai Jie; tel: 8259 0040; daily 9.30am–11.30pm; $$
This hip café is one of a chain named after the personal journal of the Russian filmmaker Andrei Tarkovsky. It serves coffee and light meals in a cultured atmosphere. A nice spot to observe hip Chinese youth. Free WiFi.

Avenue of Stone Figures human representation

THE MING TOMBS AND THE GREAT WALL AT MUTIANYU

An excursion that combines a rich encounter with Ming-dynasty history at the Ming Tombs, a beautiful drive through the mountains and an afternoon hike on the spectacular Great Wall at Mutianyu.

> **DISTANCE:** The Ming Tombs are 50km (30 miles) north-west of Beijing; the Great Wall at Mutianyu is 70km (45 miles) north-east of Beijing.
> **TIME:** A full day
> **START:** The Ming Tombs
> **END:** The Great Wall at Mutianyu
> **POINTS TO NOTE:** Consider hiring a taxi for the day to take in both major sites. Otherwise, take the subway to Nanshao station then a 10km (6-mile) taxi journey to Dagongmen to see the Ming Tombs. Tourist buses from Qianmen or Dongzhimen ply the Ming Tombs route, often making impromptu stops. Expect vigorous walking and climbing.

Although Beijing was the capital of five dynasties, only the tombs of Ming emperors are in relatively close proximity to the capital.

Thirteen of the 16 Ming emperors who reigned from 1368 to 1644 are buried about 50km (30 miles) north-west of Beijing, in an amphitheatre

formed by mountains on three sides. The foothills of the Yanshan Mountains form a natural entrance to the 40-sq-km (15-sq-mile) basin protected on both sides by the Dragon and Tiger Mountains, which are said to keep harmful winds away from the holy ground.

Heading north from Deshengmen Gate in the city, you retrace the route taken by the imperial dead to their final resting place. About 40km (25 miles) outside the city, you pass through **Changping**, formerly a garrison town that was partly responsible for guarding the tombs. The town has a monument to the peasant leader Li Zicheng, who led the uprising that toppled the Ming dynasty in 1644.

THE MING TOMBS

When you reach the **Ming Tombs** (Shisanling; daily 8.30am–5pm; charge), enter through the **Spirit Way** (Shendao), the path over which the dead were carried during the funeral ceremony. It begins with a white stone

Hall of Eminent Favours   *Elephant statues*

portico a few kilometres north of Changping and stretches nearly 6km (4 miles) to the gate of the central tomb. The entrance to the imperial graveyard, which covers 15.5 sq km (6 sq miles), is 500m/yds beyond the portico at the **Great Palace Gate** (Dagongmen).

Avenue of Stone Figures

Just beyond the gate is the entrance to the 7km (4-mile) **Avenue of Stone Figures ❶** (Shixiangshendao), also known as the Avenue of Ghosts. Leave your taxi and ask the driver to pick you up at the other end. Alternatively, public buses leave from a middle school down Kangfu Lu, just before you reach the Dragon and Phoenix Gate (Hongfengmen). The entire tomb complex is built according to exacting principles of Chinese geomancy, or *feng shui*, and this is well illustrated here. Looking through the archway at the southern end of the Spirit Way, you can see that it has been built to perfectly frame the mountains to the west. In fact, most doorways and archways here have been constructed with the view of what lies

beyond. Go through the archways to reach the avenue, which is lined with statues. Experts still debate the symbolism of these 24 carved stone creatures. Two of these, the *xiezhi* and *qilin*, are two varieties of the Chinese unicorn – mythical animals that may have been placed there for luck. The more familiar elephants, camels and horses are probably meant to serve the emperors in the afterlife. Beyond the animals are 12 stone human statues: four fierce-looking soldiers, four officials and four scholars.

Statue of Emperor Yongle in the Hall of Eminent Favours

Three of the 13 tombs in this area are officially open as tourist sites: Dingling, Changling and Zhaoling. This excursion takes you on a tour of all three.

Dingling

Your first stop is **Dingling** ❷ (daily 8.30am–6pm), about 10 minutes from the Avenue of the Stone Figures. This is the burial site of Emperor Wanli, who reigned 1573–1619. Wanli spent eight million silver taels on his bid for immortality, which was enough to feed a million people for 6.5 years at the time. It took 30,000 labourers six years to build the subterranean palace of five rooms with graceful arched ceilings – which were full of gold, silver, porcelain and jade treasures at one time.

To reach the vaults, cross the courtyard, climb the **Square Tower** (Fang Cheng) and follow the paths behind. The first room you enter has a pedestal that was intended for Wanli's concubines, but it was mysteriously empty when opened. According to a theory, this room was left empty for fear that repeated opening of the tomb would allow evil winds to disturb Wanli.

The next large room contains three stone altars, which were pushed up against the huge stone-slab doors leading to the room where the coffins of Wanli and his two wives lay along with 26 treasure chests. Some of the treasures are displayed at Changling, your next stop. More lasting is the architectural genius invested in the graves by the Ming emperors. The massive stone doors, now behind glass, were designed such that another stone slab slid into place when closed, locking them from the inside.

Zhaoling

A walkable kilometre southwest is **Zhaoling** ❸ (8.30am–5pm), the tomb of Emperor Longqing who reigned 1567–72. Longqing's short rule was characterised by liberal reform that quickly gave way to fulfilling his own personal gratifications. Three empresses were buried with him in what has become a neatly laid-out and quiet spot. Ling'en Hall was used for sacrificial ceremonies and some items remain on display.

Changling

Move on to **Changling** ❹ (daily 8.30am–5.30pm), a five-minute drive northwest of Dingling. Public buses 314 and 72 serve the route. The burial place of Emperor Yongle, who reigned 1403–24, this is the first, largest and best preserved of all the 13 tombs.

According to traditional principles of respect for elder generations, it was in poor taste for the Ming emperors following Yongle to build themselves tombs that was larger than Yongle's, although that did not stop them from doing it. The tomb complex was well tended throughout the Ming dynasty, but the Qing rulers had little motivation to care for the tombs of other

Burial paraphernalia on exhibit at Changling

dynasties, and the disrepair visible today was mostly incurred during the Qing dynasty.

Changling is a good example of how the tombs were organised. In the front section, a large courtyard dominated by twisted pines leads to a sacrificial hall. The **Hall of Eminent Favours** (Ling'endian) is supported by 32 giant pillars, each carved from a single tree. The dragon-head drains and yellow glazed tiles symbolise imperial majesty. A funeral tablet used to be placed on a wooden altar in the centre of the room, and sacrifices were made before it. The hall now contains an exhibition of items found in Dingling, including jewelled hairpins, suits of armour and the rich dragon brocade that was used in imperial dress.

The second section of Changling is a courtyard, in which a large stele marks the emperor's grave. Just behind it is the burial mound, enclosed by a wall about 500m/yds long. Presumably, this mound contains Yongle's coffin and burial treasures. To the east and the west are burial grounds for his 16 concubines who, by some accounts, were buried alive, so that they could serve and bring pleasure to Yongle in the next world.

MUTIANYU

In the far corner of the car park in Changling, 100m/yds from the entrance, is a sign in Chinese that says 'Great Wall at Mutianyu 37km'. The drive to the **Great Wall at Mutianyu** ❺ (daily 6.30am–6.30pm; charge, cable car extra) is a beautiful one eastwards through villages and mountains. Mutianyu is slightly further from Beijing than

Tourists climbing the Wall's steep steps

the crowded Badaling section, but it is well worth the journey. As you approach the Great Wall, you pass the **Schoolhouse Canteen**, see ❶. If you are feeling peckish, this is the time to stop. If you are taking public transport from the city, board tourist bus 6 from Xuanwumen.

You will spot the Great Wall long before you reach it. Adding together all the sections, the wall extends more than 3,860km (2,400 miles), though some sources may exaggerate its true length, twisting and doubling back from the coast to the north-western province of Gansu. Chinese tourist brochures assert that this is the only man-made structure visible from space (though even China's first astronaut Yang Liwei said he couldn't catch a glimpse from orbit). Whatever

The wall at Mutianyu

the case, The Great Wall is a terrific lookout point for a soldier, or a tourist.

Rise and fall of the Wall

The Great Wall is more than a remnant of history. It is also the symbol of the tyranny of imperial rule, the application of mass labour, the ingenuity of engineers and the human desire to build for immortality.

The 'Ten Thousand Li Great Wall', or *Wanli Changcheng* in Mandarin, marked the peak of wall building in China. It is misleading to speak of just one wall. The Great Wall originated as a labyrinth of smaller walls built by warring kingdoms in northern China from 5th century BC. These walls served as fortifications against plundering nomadic tribes from the north. The first Qin emperor, Shi Huangdi, after unifying China in 221 BC, made it his mission to link the walls to create a single Great Wall that would defend the country against the nomads. An army of 300,000 labourers is said to have constructed the wall under the leadership of General Meng Tian. In those days, the wall began in the west at Lintao, to the south of Lanzhou, and ran eastwards through the Inner Mongolia, Shaanxi and Hebei provinces, ending in the east of what is now Liaoning.

Wall of Bones

Just as was the case for the Egyptian pyramids, the construction of the wall

A pavilion at the Great Wall   *A viewing point*

had its dark, sinister side. Many of the peasants who were conscripted died in the process of wall building. As the many raids and later the full-scale Mongol invasion proved, the wall was only as strong as those who defended it. Nevertheless, once the Yuan dynasty was overthrown, wall building resumed with a vengeance. During the Ming period, the Great Wall really took shape. Mutianyu and most of the other remaining sections date from the Ming dynasty, when the wall was extensively repaired and fortified, and several new sections were added.

Climbing Mutianyu

Mutianyu was not part of the main wall but was a barrier shielding passes to the north towards Zhangjiakou. Its high crenellated parapets are part of the Ming-dynasty renovations completed in 1569. The restored Mutianyu section opened in 1986. The steep walk up the wall takes a good 20 minutes, but you can avoid this by taking the cable car. That might be best if you're easily winded: the steepest part of Mutianyu, a 100m/yd stretch that is more like a ladder than a stairway, named haohanpo, or 'real-man slope'.

Huanghuacheng and Simatai

Mutianyu is not the only place to climb the wall. A half-hour's drive west of Mutianyu is the section formerly known as the 'Wild Wall', **Huanghuacheng**, which has recently been restored. Much further to the north and the east, nearly in Hebei province, is **Simatai**, which also has a cable car for the less hiking-inclined. Simatai shows the unrestored Great Wall at its most majestic, crowning a narrow ridge and sharp pinnacles. To get to Huanghuacheng or Simatai, it is best to join a tour.

There are also many other 'unofficial' wall sites, though rules forbidding walking on unrenovated sections of the wall have been more strictly enforced in recent years.

The journey back to Beijing heads 75km (46 miles) south, entering the city at Dongzhimen.

Food and drink

❶ SCHOOLHOUSE CANTEEN
Off Jingcheng Expressway, just before Mutianyu (see www.theschool houseatmutianyu.com for map and directions); tel: 6162 6506; daily 10am–6pm; $$
This rather unlikely spot is a full restaurant and folk-arts centre, serving a mix of Italian and Chinese food in beautiful courtyard dining areas. The Schoolhouse can also arrange wall tours, homestays, arts and crafts activities and more. Stop by for a quick lunch before you head up the wall, or linger around for recommendations.

Hills surround Cuandixia

CUANDIXIA

Two-and-a-half hours outside of Beijing city, Cuandixia is one of the best-preserved ancient villages in the greater Beijing area. Dating from the Ming dynasty, it is a remarkably clear window onto the past.

DISTANCE: Cuandixia is 90km (56 miles) west of Beijing; the route itself covers 3–4km (2–2.5 miles), depending on how much walking you do.
TIME: A full day, or overnight
START AND END: You can simply explore the town itself, or head out for longer walks in the hills.
POINTS TO NOTE: Short of driving or taking a very expensive taxi, the best way to and from Cuandixia is by bus. Take the subway to the Pingguoyuan stop, at the end of Line 1. From there, take the twice-daily (7.30am and 12.30pm) bus No. 929 directly to Cuandixia. The bus returns to Beijing at 10am and 3pm. Expect the bus to take about 3 hours each way. Avoid going on a weekend if you don't want to meet too many tourists.

For a complete change of pace from Beijing's noisy bustle, **Cuandixia** is an excellent choice. This village was built more than 500 years ago, during the Ming Emperor Yongle's reign, and most of its buildings date back to the Ming or Qing dynasties. It is tiny, nestled on a hillside in a narrow pass, and consists of less than a hundred grey stone courtyard homes.

This village was originally a way-station between Beijing and Shanxi province to the west during the Ming dynasty. The trip was once a whole day's ride on a horse, and travellers would stay over in the villagers' homes before continuing their journey. The village was also privileged to supply the imperial palace with goats – goat herders can still be seen in the hills today.

Tranquil village

At the end of the Cultural Revolution there were a number of ancient villages scattered around the hills in the Beijing area, but the economic development of the 1980s and 1990s transformed most of them. A story has it that a group of painters from Beijing fell in love with Cuandixia. They talked to the village head, who was amenable to the idea of preservation, and some private money was found in Beijing for repairs. In 1995, Cuandixia

Drying corn   *Grey stone courtyard houses of Cuandixia*

became a tourist facility. All reconstruction and repairs are now done according to traditional building methods.

Yet despite its tourist status, it feels remarkably untouristy. There is an entrance fee and a tourist kiosk of sorts, but there are no touts or vendors, and none of the sense of being hustled that makes other tourist locations unpleasant. There are no, or few, cheesy reproductions and dioramas, and no one tries to sell you anything. The villagers, relaxed and chatty, are nevertheless dependent on tourism, and nearly every home in the village is open for meals. It's the only dining option here; just put your head into a door and ask if the family is making lunch, and expect most dishes to cost around 10–15 yuan. And if you happen to miss the last bus back to Beijing, there are plenty of people who are more than happy to put you up.

There is actually very little to do in Cuandixia, but this is part of its charm. Besides wandering the narrow alleyways, inspecting homes and old millstones, you can go for walks in the surrounding hills, which provide excellent views of the village and the environs, particularly the mountain trail on the southern side. The Beijing Hikers (www.beijinghikers.com) organise guides and accommodation to The Great Wall for small groups.

DOUBLE-STONE VILLAGE

As you approach Cuandixia's gate, you pass through a small, run-down village named **Double-Stone Village** (Shuangshitou), also of great age. To some, this may be of more interest than Cuandixia itself – it is of comparable age to its larger neighbour, but for whatever reason, it has escaped the blessing of the tourism bureau. The village, dependent on now-exhausted coal mines, is crumbling. A good number of the courtyard houses are completely abandoned, and the villagers are much older on average. The locals here are not quite as cheerful as Cuandixia's – with good reason – but if you're friendly and considerate, they are happy to take you in and talk with you. They have very long memories.

The Mountain Manor for Escaping the Summer Heat is set amidst the Yunshan Mountains

CHENGDE

An overnight stay at the eclectic mountain retreat of Qing emperors.
Explore the manor, its museum and a labyrinth of paths, bridges,
pavilions, halls and temples surrounding several interlocking lakes.

DISTANCE: 250km (150 miles) east of Beijing; 4 hours by train. Day 1:is 2.6km (1.6 miles); Day 2: is 5.3km (3.3 miles)
TIME: Consider staying for two or even three days to see everything in Chengde. It can take a day just to see the Chengde temples.
START: Bishu Shanzhuang
END: Club Peak
POINTS TO NOTE: Daily trains leave from Beijing North, Beijing East and Beijing Station. The quickest and most convenient is the K7711 from Beijing Station departing at 8.05am and arriving in Chengde at 12.31am. You can return to Beijing by hourly coaches that leave from the long distance bus station next to the railway station. The journey takes about five hours. In Chengde, walking from sight to sight is not very practical; hire a taxi or rent a bicycle for the day.

Emperor Kangxi of the Qing dynasty was drawn to the town of Chengde, capital of the former province Jehol, because of its location in a cool, lush valley with placid lakes and forests, 350m (1,150ft) above sea level. He ordered the building of the **Mountain Manor for Escaping the Summer Heat** (Bishu shanzhuang; daily 5.30am–6.30pm; charge) in 1703, which turned the previously obscure town into an imperial resort with a regal garden that was the largest in China. Remnants of it can still be viewed today. The manor was also used in the later years of the Qing dynasty, when Emperor Qianlong expanded the residence, incorporating the styles of China's minorities in his sprawling retreat as part of an effort to appease them.

For over a century, emperors and their retinues enjoyed summer hunting expeditions in Chengde. But after 1820, when a bolt of lightning killed Emperor Jiaqing, who was in residence here, the resort was abandoned. Xianfeng was the only emperor ever to stay here again, when he was forced to flee Beijing during the Second Opium War in 1860.

Around Chengde

If you have just one night in Chengde, spend the first afternoon strolling

The Goddess of Mercy in the Temple of Universal Peace

through Bishu Shanzhuang and save the more strenuous exploration of the temples for the next morning. In the Yanshan Mountains that surround the resort were 12 active temples, varying in architectural styles. Of the 12, only eight were in good enough condition to warrant renovation, and two of those are still closed to the public. The buildings and gardens cover a total area of 560 hectares (1,400 acres) and are surrounded by a wall 10km (6 miles) long.

If you have more time, bizarre rock formations, caves and hot springs await in the outlying areas. Chengde is quite compact and Bishu Shanzhuang can be reached easily on foot from the

hotels. Public buses and minibuses also run up the main road, Wulie Lu, and stop next to the main gate (Lizhengmen) of Bishu Shanzhuang.

Little in Chengde is translated for non-Chinese speakers. You may want to hire a guide through the local branch of the **China International Travel Service** (CITS; 11 Zhonghua Lu; tel: 0314-202 6418), or try haggling with the guides who sell their services at Bishu Shanzhuang.

MANOR MUSEUM

Start just inside the main gate, at the **Bishushanzhuang Museum ❶** (Bishushanzhuang Bowuguan; daily 7.30am–5.30pm; charge), which once housed the main palace. Laid out in the traditional linear style of halls and courtyards, it is made of unpainted wood and shaded by tall pines. The exhibits are varied: some rooms display items like Mongolian weapons and dress, others are set up as they were when they were used by the imperial court. Leave by the back door of the museum to get to the park proper. Surrounded by a 10km (6 mile) wall, it is the largest-surviving imperial garden in China.

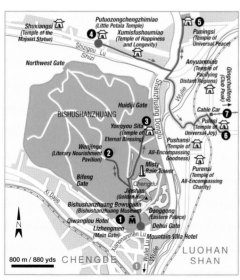

Tibetan architecture of Little Potala Temple

PAVILIONS AND TEMPLES

On the right, after 100m/yds, begins a maze of paths, bridges, pavilions and halls surrounding several lakes. This area is perfect for strolls, boating and relaxing. Beyond it is the **Literary Nourishment Pavilion ❷** (Wenjinge), one of four imperial libraries. Its central attraction is a rock garden where there is a special place for permanently 'viewing the moon', a trick of light falling on the surrounding rock formations. At the far end of the east side of the park, there is a meadow marked by the pagoda of the **Temple of Eternal Blessing ❸** (Yongyou Sita), which was built by Emperor Qianlong for his mother's 50th birthday.

Heading left from the lake, you come to a more rugged hiking area. Emperors Kangxi and Qianlong designated 72 scenic spots in Bishu Shanzhuang, but you can find many more. The hills are riddled with small temples and rock formations and topped by pavilion lookout points. A good place to enjoy the greenery is the tea garden at the south-eastern corner of Front Lake, the main lake.

Each of the temples around the city has its own admission fee, which can make a trip to all the temples add up.

OUTER TEMPLES

Get an early start on your second day and head for the temples beyond the walls of Bishu Shanzhuang. A good way to do this is to rent a taxi for the morning or day. Hiring a bicycle is also a good idea; you can visit a selection of temples, and the scenery on your ride is excellent. A number of hotels, including Yunshan Hotel, rent out bicycles. The full circuit comprises the **Eight Outer Temples**, but start with these four (below) and see how your time and energy hold out.

Little Potala Temple
Little Potala Temple ❹ (Putuozongchengzhimiao; daily 8.30am–5pm), which dates from 1767, is the largest and most spectacular complex, modelled on the Potala Palace in Lhasa, Tibet. The beautifully restored halls, staircases and walkways extend over a 22-hectare (54-acre) hillside site. Tibetan-style prayer flags, banners and tapestries hang from the gleaming gold roofs of the temple. The design of the **Temple of Happiness and Longevity** (Xumifushoumiao; daily 8am–5.30pm), 1km (0.6 mile) east, is based on another Tibetan temple, at Shigatse. At its rear is one of the highlights, an octagonal pagoda that commemorates the 70th birthday of Emperor Qianlong.

Temple of Universal Peace
The **Temple of Universal Peace ❺** (Puningsi; daily 8.30am–5pm), 3km (2 miles) further north-east and built in 1755, stands out as it is a living monastery with some 50 lamas in residence. The second hall is laid out with long, low benches for religious study and cere-

Gates to Little Potala Temple

Buddhist statue carved on the Liuli–Wanshou pagoda

mony. There is an amazing 22-m (72-ft) carved wooden statue of Guanyin, the Goddess of Mercy, said to be the largest wooden statue in the world. Also known as the Thousand-Arm, Thousand-Eye Guanyin, the statue has 42 arms and an eye on each palm, signifying her inexhaustible power of salvation.

Temple of Universal Joy

Finally, move on to the **Temple of Universal Joy** ❻ (Pulesi; daily 8am–6pm), which lies east of Bishu Shanzhuang. This was built in 1766 in honour of Kazhak, Kirghiz and other nobles from north-western China. The complex is similar in style to the main hall of the Temple of Heaven in Beijing. Its main building, the round Pavilion of Morning Light (Xuguangge), sits on a square terrace, symbolising Heaven and Earth, respectively, according to ancient Chinese cosmology. In the pavilion are bronze images of the deities in various acts of passionate embrace and conquest of their enemies – great examples of the wonderful but terrifying imagery in Tibetan Buddhism.

CLUB PEAK

One of the strangest rock formations in the area is at **Club Peak** ❼ (Qingchuifeng). The legend behind the peak says that it was formed when a monk and a local spirit fought, and the monk's club was turned to stone. At the top of a sloping hill, the stone does look very much like a vast club, balanced precariously on its narrow end. You can get there by taking a cable car a few hundred metres north of the Temple of Universal Joy. It is possible to ascend to the platform on which the stone stands, though, of course, it is impossible to mount the stone itself.

Accommodation and food

There are a few good places to stay in Chengde, such as the four-star **Yunshan Hotel** (2 Banbishan Lu; tel: 0314-205 5588) and **Qiwanglou Hotel** (1 Bifengmen Donglu; tel: 0314-202 4385), a reproduction of a Qing-dynasty mansion

Local cuisine centres mainly on wild game, as the area was traditionally reserved as the emperors' hunting ground. Try **Huanggong Yushanfang**, see ❶, at the Palace Hotel.

Food and drink

❶ HUANGGONG YUSHANFANG

Palace Hotel, 21 Wulie Lu; tel: 0314-206 2688; daily 8.30am–9.30pm; $$$

This period-style restaurant is a bit of a pageant show but it does give a sense of history. Women dressed as Qing-dynasty imperial maids serve venison, wild boar and pheasant – the food emperors ate – along with more humble Chinese fare. Ask for prices in advance; they are not listed on the menu. Reservations are advised.

DIRECTORY

Hand-picked hotels and restaurants to suit all budgets and tastes, organised by area, plus select nightlife listings, an alphabetical listing of practical information, a language guide and an overview of the best books and films to give you a flavour of the city.

ACCOMMODATION

In recent years, Beijing has experienced a boom in hotel construction, with some spectacular new or refurbished five-star establishments, as well as an increase in the number of lower-end hotels and hostels. There are also a large number of very comfortable mid-range hotels, which can offer good value and good facilities. A recent development has been the growth in smaller boutique hotels and old-style courtyard hotels, full of period features.

Rates at all but the budget hotels are subject to 10–15 percent tax and service charge. It is advisable to book in advance during the peak tourist season (June to October). At other times, hotels may offer discounts or special packages; be sure to ask for a discount no matter when you are booking. Most accept reservations from abroad online or by fax.

Fragrant Hills and Western Suburbs

Aman at the Summer Palace
1 Gongmenqian Jie, Haidian; tel: 5987 9999; www.amanresorts.com; $$$$

> Price for a standard double room for one night:
> $$$$ = US$200 and above
> $$$ = US$150–200
> $$ = US$100–150
> $ = US$50–100

Housed in over a square kilometre of courtyards and pavilions that were once a waiting area for imperial audiences, the 51 rooms at the Aman at the Summer Palace resort are Beijing's best bet at experiencing imperial pampering. Beyond the devoted service and period-fixture rooms, guests have access to amenities like an subterranean spa and three fine-dining restaurants, as well as a private entrance into the park to tour the Summer Palace before the tourists arrive.

Fragrant Hills Hotel
Inside Fragrant Hills Park; tel: 6259 1166; fax: 6259 1762; www.xsfd.com; $$
A modern sanctuary in the lush hills north-west of Beijing, beyond the Summer Palace. Designed by the world-renowned architect I.M. Pei, this hotel is one of the more successful meldings of Eastern and Western styles in Beijing. With a swimming pool and Chinese and Western restaurants.

Friendship Hotel
1 Nandajie, Zhongguancun; tel: 6849 8888; www.bjfriendshiphotel.com; $$
Part of a huge, state-run hotel spread out in pleasant grounds close to the Summer Palace and the university district, the hotel has several sections offering a range of prices and facilities. The hotel was built in 1954, and at

An iconic place to stay in Beijing

one time it was the only place in Beijing where foreigners were allowed to live. It is still home to many foreigners working for Chinese state employers.

Presidential Plaza

9 Fuchengmenwai Lu, Xicheng; tel: 5858 5588; www.presidentialplazahotelbeijing. cn; $$$

A modern addition to the Diaoyutai State Guest House, this has less stringent security and more contemporary facilities, though it still has a definite air of government sponsorship. All 502 rooms have high-speed internet access and multiple phone lines.

Royal Garden Hotel

Shuizha Beilu, Mentougou; tel: 6984 3366/ 3362; www.lqhotel.com; $$

For atmosphere and facilities, this international hotel, built in classical Chinese style, beats most similarly priced hotels in the city. The only disadvantage is that it is located near the Western Hills, about an hour from the city centre. Its beautiful traditional Chinese garden, though, makes excellent use of the suburban surrounds.

Shangri-La Hotel

29 Zizhuyuan Lu, Haidian; tel: 6841 2211; www.shangri-la.com; $$

This tasteful high-rise hotel has meeting rooms, a ballroom, French and Asian restaurants and a full range of other facilities. On the western edge of the city, it provides a shuttle bus service to downtown areas. Chi claims to be the most luxurious spa in Beijing. Shuttle boat services run regularly to the Summer Palace.

Wangfujing and the Foreign Legation Quarter

Beijing Hotel

33 Dongchang'an Jie, Dongcheng; tel: 6513 7766; www.chinabeijinghotel. cn; $$$$

Opened in 1917 and recently refurbished, with a long list of famous guests, this is the grande dame of Beijing hotels – its period features give it an air of tradition, in contrast to many newer competitors. It was chosen as the official home of the Olympic Committee for the 2008 Olympic Games. Centrally located, on the corner of Wangfujing Dajie shopping street and five minutes from Tiananmen Square.

Dongjiaominxiang Hotel

23A Dongjiaomin Xiang, Dongcheng; tel: 6524 3311; www.cbw.com/hotel/bj-dongjiaominxiang; $$

This business hotel may not have remarkable rooms, but it does have a great location – in the atmospheric Foreign Legation Quarter, on Dongxiaomin Xiang, two minutes from Tiananmen Square and 10 minutes from Wangfujing Dajie shopping street. The Gold Harbour Seafood restaurant is an excellent spot for Chaozhou and Cantonese fare, and a rooftop Western-style club offers great views.

Hilton Beijing Wangfujing pool

Fangyuan Hotel

36 Dengshikou Xijie, Dongcheng; tel: 6525 6331; fax: 6513 8549; $

The two-star Fangyuan Hotel may not be particularly smart, but its location just off Wangfujing Dajie and opposite the former home of Lao She, an important 20th-century writer, plus its range of inexpensive rooms, make it worth considering. Breakfast is included.

Grand Hyatt

1 Dongchang'an Jie, Dongcheng; tel: 8518 1234; www.beijing.grand.hyatt.com; $$$$

This first-rate hotel is ensconced in the impressive Oriental Plaza complex. Its enormous concave facade is a landmark of Chang'an Jie. Beijing's premier shopping street, Wangfujing Dajie, is next door and the Forbidden City is just a stroll away. The hotel has an excellent choice of restaurants – Noble Court is one of the better spots in town for Cantonese food, and the Red Moon lounge has a good selection of whiskies.

Haoyuan Hotel

53 Shijia Hutong, Dongsi Nandajie, Dongcheng; tel: 6512 5557; $

Hidden away in a narrow alleyway near the busy Dongdan shopping street, Haoyuan is housed in Qing-era courtyard buildings that feature a traditional combination of brick and red lacquered wood, with curved tiles on the roofs. Rooms, with antique-style furnishings, are clustered around the courtyards, and a small restaurant serves hearty traditional fare at very reasonable prices.

Hilton Beijing Wangfujing

8 Wangfujing Dongjie, Dongcheng; tel: 5812 8888; www3.hilton.com; $$$

While a little bit worse for wear, the Hilton Wangfujing boasts the deluxe accommodations expected of the international brand. The central location a short walk from Tiananmen Square makes it ideal for visitors new in town, and the hotel's restaurant Chynna serves well-regarded Peking Duck. West-facing rooms above the 10th floor have views of the Forbidden City.

Lee Garden Service Apartments

18 Jinyu Hutong, Wangfujing Dajie; tel: 6525 8855; www.lgapartment.com; $$$

This is a good option for long-term stays or if you'd like to have a kitchen and other home comforts. The suites range in size from studio to three-room. This 199-room serviced apartment also offers childcare and a children's play area. Some rooms have balconies with a view of the Forbidden City.

Novotel Peace Hotel

3 Jinyu Hutong, Dongcheng; tel: 6512 8833; www.novotel.com; $$

This is a smart and modern four-star hotel with a central location just off Wangfujing Dajie. Its French restaurant, Le Cabernet, is popular for its extensive wine cellar, and often hosts events for Beijing's French community.

Old–world charm of the Raffles Beijing

The Peninsula

8 Jinyu Hutong, Wangfujing Dajie, Dongcheng; tel: 8516 2888; www.penninsula.com/beijing $$$$

A modern, functional hotel with Chinese imperial flourishes and tastefully designed rooms. A waterfall cascades down to a lobby full of Chinese antiques, while designer labels fill the shopping arcade. One of the hotel's restaurants Jing has drawn notice for its fusion cuisine.

Raffles Beijing Hotel

33 Dongchang'an Jie, Dongcheng; tel: 6526 3388; beijing.raffles.com; $$$$

Occupying the same block as Beijing Hotel, this lavish hotel comes with all the luxuries and mod cons expected of the Raffles brand. Its 171 rooms and suites, including some 'personality suites' named after luminaries who had been hosted in them, such as Sun Yat-sen and Henri Cartier-Bresson, blend old-world Oriental elegance with contemporary amenities. Its acclaimed restaurant Jaan serves exquisite modern French cuisine.

The Temple Hotel

23 Shatan Beijie, Dongcheng; tel: 8401 5680; www.thetemplehotel.com; $$$$

Belgian expat Juan van Wassenhove renovated a 600-year-old Buddhist temple complex nearby the Forbidden City from ruin to a truly unique Beijing destination. The eight rooms – spacious former monks' quarters – are located around a UNESCO-recognized great hall, modern art is tastefully placed throughout, and the antique decorations in the rooms are mixed with helpful technology and fawning service. Listen carefully, and you may awake to birdsong, a beautiful rarity in Beijing.

Lake District

Beijing Backpackers Hostel

85 Nanluogu Xiang, Dongcheng; tel: 8400 2429; www.backpackingchina.com; $

A hostel located in a *hutong* in Jiaodaokou, right in the middle of the Nanluogu Xiang café and bar scene, and within walking distance of Houhai. This is cleaner and better run than some of the more established hostels in the area, and has also become an information exchange for backpackers travelling to other parts of China. It organises tours to sights such as the Great Wall.

Beijing Bamboo Garden Hotel

24 Xiaoshiqiao Hutong, Jiugulou Dajie; tel: 6403 2229; www.bbgh.com.cn; $

Simple, clean rooms open out to a classical Chinese garden. What it lacks in facilities compared with large, modern hotels, it more than compensates for in atmosphere. Multiple courtyards and its location in a *hutong* offer more peace and quiet than you are likely to find anywhere else in Beijing. The location, close to the Drum Tower, is slightly inconvenient, but that is part of the charm.

Double Happiness Beijing Courtyard Hotel

37 Dongsi Sitiao, Dongcheng; tel: 6400 7762; www.doublehappiness courtyard.com; $

This charming courtyard hotel, with chinoiserie furniture and Chinese-style bedding, gives a memorably local experience. Be warned: a lack of adequate heating and small bathrooms might make for a less happy experience in winter.

Lama Temple International Youth Hostel

56 Wudaoying Hutong, Dongcheng; tel: 6400 8515; $

A well-designed hostel only steps from the Lama Temple and Gui Jie restaurant street that makes an excellent starting point for those exploring the hutongs.

Lusongyuan Hotel

22 Banchang Hutong, Kuanjie, Dongcheng; tel: 6404 0436; www.cbw.com/hotel/lusongyuan; $

This hotel was established in 1980 in the courtyard residence of a former Qing-dynasty official. Stone lions still guard the traditional wooden gate, which leads to the pavilions, trees, rockeries and potted plants that fill the courtyards. The rooms are refined and airy. Great location in a Jiaodaokou *hutong*, and a good breakfast spot even if you are not staying there.

The Orchid

65 Baochao Hutong, Dongcheng; Tel: 8404 4818; www.theorchidbeijing.com; $$

Hidden down a nondescript alley, this serene courtyard hotel is tailor-made for an authentic hutong experience while keeping every ounce of comfort. Each of the 10 smart, sunlit rooms in the lovingly restored Qing dynasty-era house have rain showers, goose-down beds and complementary local tea, while the more expensive suites have private terraces and thoughtful additions like pre-programmed cell phones. Serviced apartments are also available for long-term stays.

Chaoyang and the CBD

Beijing International Hotel

9 Jianguomennei Dajie, Dongcheng; tel: 6512 6688; www.bih.com.cn; $$

With a good location near the Beijing Railway Station and Henderson and Cofco Plaza shopping centres, this 1,000-room hotel offers a full range of facilities, including a booking office for international flights and trains. The Starlight Revolving Restaurant provides stunning views of the city. This is a popular spot for international conventions.

China World Hotel

1 Jianguomenwai Dajie, Chaoyang East; tel: 6505 2266; www.shangri-la.com; $$$$

Top-class service and accommodation options, with a health club, swimming pool, and shopping and business centres. Its restaurants include Aria, a well-known spot for seafood and wine, and Scene a Café, good for business lunches. It is well located for business

travellers, and provides access to extensive business and conference facilities.

East, Beijing

22 Jiuxianqiao Lu, Chaoyang; tel: 0426 0888; www.east-beijing.com; $$$$
This 25-storey lifestyle business hotel has comfortable, well-appointed rooms and a location easily reachable from the airport, making it a good option for short-term travellers who want to see a little more of the city. It's linked to a huge mall, business and fitness centres are on site, and the two restaurants and enormous three-level bar win praise.

Gloria Plaza Hotel

2 Jianguomen Nandajie, Chaoyang East; tel: 6515 8855; www.gphbeijing.com; $$$
Gloria Plaza has a great location on a major junction, opposite the Ancient Observatory and next to one of the main CITS offices. Rooms on the higher floors provide excellent views of the city. There are several restaurants and an American-style sports bar, Sports City Café, which is almost over the top in its homage to basketball.

Grace Hotel

Jiuxianqiao Beilu, 2 Hao Yuan, Chaoyang; tel: 6436 1818; $$$
This elegant stay is the only accommodation in 798, but it fits so well it might be mistaken for one of the galleries. Guests are greeted with seasonal exhibitions in the lobby, lots of prints in the rooms and an insider's guide to current shows in the art district. The hotel's restaurant Yi House has top-notch European fare.

Hotel Éclat

9 Dongdaqiao Lu, Chaoyang; tel: 8561 2888; www.eclathotels.com/beijing; $$$$
Owned by a Hong Kong billionaire who displays his private art collection of original Warhols and Dalis around the hotel, the 100-room Hotel Eclat mixes quirky design – massage chairs, 3-D televisions, lamps controlled by laser gun – with decadent luxury. Big spenders can apply for rooms themed like 'Star Wars' or 'Alice in Wonderland', and some suites have private pools, There's no chic eateries to match the modish surrounds, but the hotel is linked to a luxury mall with some of Beijing's finest restaurants.

Jingguang New World Hotel

Hujia Lou, Dongsanhuan Lu (East Third Ring Road), Chaoyang East; tel: 6597 8888; www.jingguangcentre.com; $$
A 53-storey building on the eastern Third Ring Road, the Jingguang New World is almost a self-contained town, with its own bakery, restaurants, nightclubs, children's play areas, medical centre and supermarket – and, of course, some of the best views of Beijing.

Kempinski Hotel Lufthansa Centre

50 Liangmaqiao Lu, Beijing Lufthansa Centre, Chaoyang Northeast; tel: 6465 3388; www.kempinski-beijing.com; $$$

Attached to the Youyi (Friendship) Shopping City, the Kempinski has all the facilities and amenities a discerning traveller could ask for, including a health club and the pub and restaurant Paulaner Brauhaus, which serves great German beer and cuisine. The hotel is also extremely convenient for access to airline offices and the Women's Street bar district.

Kerry Centre

1 Guanghua Lu (opposite the north gate of China World Trade Centre), Chaoyang; tel: 6561 8833; www.shangri-la.com; $$$$

Aimed at business travellers and linked to a major commercial and shopping complex, the Kerry Centre offers a full range of facilities, from jacuzzis to live-jazz performances, from movie channels to broadband internet access. A new children's fun-zone, with two slides and a massive playground, is perfect for families with small children.

Opposite House

11 Sanlitun Lu, Chaoyang; tel: 6417 6688; www.theoppositehouse.com; $$

This impossibly fashionable Japanese-designed hotel is one of the most stylish spots in town. The lobby seems more like a work of art and the rooms are a minimalist's dream. Two bars and three restaurants are on site.

Red Capital Club Residence

9 Dongsi Liutiao, Dongcheng; tel: 8403 5308; www.redcapitalclub.com.cn; $$$

One of the most exclusive in Beijing, this boutique property is set in a renovated courtyard building that is companion to the Red Capital Club restaurant three *hutongs* north. Sip wine in a former bomb shelter beneath the hotel's five suites, each with its own historical theme. Kitschy Communist paraphernalia are scattered around the hotel.

Sanlitun Youth Hostel

1 Chunxiu Lu, Chaoyang; 5190 9288; www.sanlitun.hostel.com; $

Located a short walk to the Sanlitun bar street, this backpacker hostel is good value for money, especially for those looking for a few boozy nights out. Sleeping conditions are average, though a fun hostel bar, decent food and a convivial traveller atmosphere might make up for it. Friendly staff can help you organise a trip out to the Great Wall.

St Regis

21 Jianguomenwai Dajie, Chaoyang East; tel: 6460 6688; www.stregis.com/beijing; $$$$

This marvellous and centrally located five-star hotel impresses with an elegant foyer, fine restaurants and a high standard of luxury – the amount of marble in the lobby alone is shocking. Its Press Club Bar is a long-time favourite of the expat business community, while its spa and massage facilities are top-notch.

Traders Hotel suite

Traders Hotel

1 Jianguomenwai Dajie, Chaoyang East; tel: 6505 2277; www.shangri-la.com; $$$

Well located at the northern end of the China World Trade Centre business complex, the Traders has excellent food, service and accommodation. As it is less expensive than its neighbour, the China World Hotel, the Traders is good for business travellers who are looking for comfort but not top-flight luxury.

Southern Beijing

Kelly's Courtyard

25 Xiaoyuan Hutong, Xidan Beidajie; tel: 6611 8515; www.kellyscoutryard.com; $$

This is a small courtyard hotel with rooms that are pleasantly decorated and a nice communal area.

Leo Hostel

52 Dazhilan Xijie; tel: 6303 1595; www.leo hostel.com; $

Friendly, bustling hostel on Dazhalan Street offering various tour bookings for travellers, including a popular trip to a 'secret' section of the Great Wall.

pentahotel

3-18 Chongwenmen Wadajie, Dongcheng; tel: 6708 1188; www.pentahotels.com; $$

The pentahotel (yes, with a little 'p') tries its darndest to be a warm counterpart to the familiar, staid Chinese hotel package. There's not much in the surrounding area, though the hotel lends out bikes to guests for an easy ride to the nearby Temple of Heaven or Tiananmen Square. Rooms are simple, but comfortable, and the hotel sports a lounge instead of a lobby and a few good Chinese restaurants.

Great Wall

Commune by the Great Wall

Great Wall Exit at Shuiguan, Badaling Highway; tel: 8118 1888; www.commune.com.cn; $$$$

Twelve spectacular villas – with equally spectacular prices and views – designed by Asia's top architects. Each villa has many bedrooms and a personal butler.

Chengde

Chengde Hotel

19 Nanyingzi Dajie; tel: 0314-590 1888; $$

This is probably the classiest hotel in the area, located right in the heart of town, with easy access to sights and transport, and is as close as Chengde comes to luxury.

Mongolian Yurt Holiday Village

Tel: 0314-216 3094; $

Economical and kitschy yurts (containing TVs, washrooms and air-conditioning) are available within the grounds of the imperial resort.

Qiwanglou Hotel

1 Bifengmen Lu; tel: 0314-202 4385; $$

For its atmosphere alone, this hotel is the best option you can find in Chengde. The small but exquisite hotel occupies a Qing-dynasty mansion, set just inside the grounds of the imperial resort.

Peking duck

RESTAURANTS

American

Big Smoke Bistro

Lee World Building, 57 Xingfucun Zhong Lu, Chaoyang; tel: 6416 5195; 11am–midnight Mon-Sat, 11am–10pm Sun; $$

This contemporary American joint adds flair to the backyard barbecue known for monster burgers, truffle-oil macaroni and cheese and an eight-hour wood-fired suckling pig that puts their mastery of the BBQ pit centre stage. Jing-A Brewing runs their craft beer operation in the back.

Kro's Nest

35 Xiaoyun Lu, Chaoyang; tel: 8391 3131; www.krosnest.com; daily 11am-midnight; $$

Thick-crust, American-style pizza that comes in gargantuan sizes, as well as frosty beers, cocktails and milkshakes to help you wash it down.

Beijing

Liqun Roast Duck

11 Beixiangfeng, Zhengyi Nanlu, Qianmen Dongdajie; tel: 6705 5578; 10am–10pm; $$

Once a hidden *hutong* gem, Liqun is now an open secret, but it still serves

good Peking duck. Reservations are advised, or you'll need to wait up to an hour, as the converted courtyard home cannot seat too many. Liqun also has a good selection of family-style Chinese dishes; the owners will be happy to sit down with you and discuss your meal.

Duck De Chine

1949 The Hidden City, 4 Gongti Beilu, Chaoyang; tel: 6501 8881; daily 11.30am–2.30pm; 6–10.30pm; $$$

Without a doubt, Duck de Chine is the city's most glamorous location for Peking Duck. Each bird is methodically roasted over jujube wood before entering the dining room at the sound of a gong. Other, non-duck, dishes are fantastic as well. Those with means (or an expense account) might consider some bubbly from the Bollinger champagne bar, the only one in China.

Siji Minfu

32 Dengshikou Xijie, Dongcheng; tel: 6513 5141; daily 10.30am–10.30pm; $$

Siji Minfu serves top-quality Peking duck without an eye-popping price tag. That bargain alone all but guarantees a packed house during mealtimes at each of its multiple locations, adding more liveliness to the Beijing-chic dining room of chirping birds and hanging lanterns. Other than duck, their diverse selection of Beijing cuisine standards is mostly on point.

> Price guide for a two-course meal for one with an alcoholic drink:
> $$$ = over 200 yuan
> $$ = 100–200 yuan
> $ = 50–100 yuan

East-meets-West concoction

Hostess at an imperial cuisine restaurant

Cantonese

East Ocean Seafood

39 Maizidian Jie, Chaoyang (near Lufthansa Centre); tel: 6508 3482; daily 11am–11pm; $$

The Cantonese clientele should be your first clue to this restaurant's authenticity and prowess. It is consistently packed, and regularly wins prizes for best Cantonese food in Beijing. It is more expensive than other restaurants, but worth it – the seafood is fresh and the dim sum is great.

Hengshan Hui

1/F, Kerry EAS Logistics Building, 21 Xiaoyun Lu, Chaoyang; tel: 6466 1211; daily 10.30am-11pm; www.hengshancafe.com.cn;$$

Solid Hong Kong teahouse staples intended for a discerning clientele, with a dim sum menu that's a step above the rest. The bustling crowd usually includes anyone from business types to extended families, meaning you should show up early if you don't want to wait.

Xian Lao Man

51 Jiugulou Dajie; tel: 6403 9907; daily 11am–11pm; $

The name translates to 'full of stuffing' and it's right on the money: locals and expats alike flock to this chain for some excellent dumplings. All dumplings are made to order, with dozens of fillings to choose from, and can be steamed or fried crispy as potstickers. There's also an encyclopaedic selection of very authentic Beijing dishes at affordable prices.

Chinese (other)

The East is Red

266 Baijialou, East Third Ring Road; tel: 6574 8289; daily 9am–2.30pm, 4–9.30pm; $$

Cultural Revolution-era nostalgia and plenty of kitsch. Watch rousing nightly performances of Communist song and dance and period fare in this truly unique restaurant. It's difficult to find so ask your taxi driver to call for directions.

Guoli Zhuang

500m/yds west of Dongsi Shitiao Bridge, Dongcheng; tel: 8411 6666; daily 11am–10pm; $$$

This restaurant is mostly known for its novelty, but what a novelty! Specialising in 'men's health food', it serves a shocking range of animal penises, cooked in a range of styles. You can try grilled deer vitals, cow testicles or a 'three-penis' hot pot if it is variety you're after. Warning: it is quite expensive.

Chongqing

Shunfeng 123

West Gate of the Workers' Stadium; tel: 6551 3123; daily 10.30am–10.30pm; $$

Chongqing food is nearly as spicy as the better known Sichuan fare. This restaurant is no exception serving up fiery pork dishes, rabbit hotpot and flavoursome green beans.

Laying tables at an upmarket restaurant

Sanyangcai
North Gate of the Worker's Stadium; tel: 6552 3499; daily 11am–11pm; $$

Sanyangcai's huge menu is a good primer to Chongqing's famously piquant cuisine. The name refers to three specialties of the region – dry-braised eels, loach with mustard greens and spicy bullfrog – which are all delicious, but it's hard to go wrong with whatever you order here. The massive dining hall has no shortage of seating.

Dongbei

Baoyuan Jiaozi Wu
6 Maizidian Jie, Chaoyang; 6586 4987; daily 11am–10pm; $

Baoyuan dyes its dumplings with vibrant colours to match their fillings, a photo-friendly gimmick that helps you tell their mounds of absolutely fantastic dumplings apart. The menu stretches from traditional favourites to off-beat combinations using crispy rice or crunchy lotus root. Feel free to stuff yourself – prices are cheap and the restaurant is very foreigner friendly.

European

Temple Restaurant Beijing
23 Shatan Beijie, Chaoyang; tel: 8400 2232; daily 11.30am–2.30pm, 6–10pm; www.trb-cn.com; $$$

Temple Restaurant Beijing is a must-try for destination fine dining in the capital. The restaurant combines old and new in a way nowhere else can: walk through a genuine Ming dynasty-era temple to a minimalist dining room serving French-inflected European cuisine. Top that with incomparable service, thanks to manager Ignace LeClair, who previously worked under culinary superstar Daniel Boulud in New York, and perhaps the city's best wine list. Their lunch deal is a good way to get the full experience on a budget.

French

Brasserie Flo
18 Xiaoyun Lu, Chaoyang; tel: 6595 5135; daily 11am–3pm and 5.30–11pm; www.flo.cn; $$$

Beijing's original French restaurant, and one of the most authentic. This brasserie sticks close to the French essentials and does them right – goose liver with apple, onion soup and imported oysters. And, of course, great French wines by the glass or bottle.

Fusion

Mosto
3/F, Nali Patio, 81 Sanlitun Lu, Chaoyang; tel: 5208 6030; Sun–Thu noon–2.30pm, 6–10pm; Fri–Sat noon–2.30pm, 6–10.30pm; www.mostobj.com; $$

Mosto has kept pace with Beijing's rapid change through consistent and creative reinvention, yet never managing to drop in quality. The current menu from serial restaurateurs Daniel Urdaneta and Alex Molina features contemporary Western dishes with a dress-down sensibility, perfect for an upscale yet casual dinner or brunch.

A chef serving up his creation

Guizhou

Dagui

69 Daxing Hutong, Dongcheng; tel: 6407 1800; daily 10am–2pm, 5–10pm; $$

Southern Guizhou cuisine is famous in China for its distinctive sour-spicy one-two combo. Few places pull that tricky balance off better than Dagui, with the hallmark suantangyu, fresh fish in a tomato, coriander, lemongrass and chilli broth. The ramshackle hutong courtyard adds a lot of homely character.

Hot Pot

Haidilao

2A Baijiazhuang Lu, Sanlitun; tel: 6595 2982; daily 24 hours; $

Hot pot, where diners cook thinly sliced meat and vegetables in a bubbling cauldron at the table, already has elements of culinary theatre. Haidilao raises it to full-blown spectacle: diners can enjoy free manicures and kid's toys while waiting in line, there's an eye-popping buffet of dipping sauces to choose from and hand-pulled noodles are served via hip-hop dance. All of this is done 24 hours a day, with famously welcoming service even in the wee hours of the morning.

Hunanese

Nice Rice

23 Dongsi Ertiao, Dongcheng; tel: 8408 4345; daily 11am-10pm; $

An eclectic selection of spicy, smoky Hunanese dishes, served in a two-floor hutong setup. It's popular with artistic types who show up for the mounds of chilli in each dish. The signature florets of sizzling cauliflower are delicious.

Yuelu Shanwu

10 Lotus Lane, Qianhai, Lake District; tel: 6617 2696; daily 11am–11pm; $

Splendid Hunanese food in a sleek setting that combines traditional and modern elements. Its outdoor seating area offers a good view of Qianhai; for privacy, reserve a room upstairs.

Imperial

Laijinyuxuan Restaurant

Zhongshan Park; tel: 6605 6676; daily 10.30am–7.30pm; $$

Housed in a building resembling a traditional garden house, this restaurant, nearly a century old, serves aristocrat cuisine described in the Qing-dynasty novel *Dream of the Red Mansions*. The *dongcai baozi* (steamed buns with preserved cabbage) is a must-try.

Li Family Restaurant (Lijia Cai)

11 Yangfang Hutong, Deshengmennei Dajie, Xicheng; tel: 6613 7509; daily 11am–1.30pm, 5–8.30pm; $$$

Totally unprepossessing, inside and out, this home restaurant serves only four tables of up to 12 seats each day. It is run by Li Shanling, who still has the books and recipes his great-grandfather, an imperial chef, left him. With them, he creates some of the best food in the country, hands down. There is no menu – you eat what he makes. World

Baozi (steamed buns)

leaders dine here regularly. Book two or three days in advance.

Indian

The Taj Pavilion

China World Trade Centre, Chaoyang; tel: 6505 5866, ext. 8116; daily 11.30am–2.30pm and 6–10.30pm; $$

Relaxed Indian restaurant with a large and convincing menu. It may be a tad expensive to eat here, but both the ambience and the dishes are excellent. Go for the lunch buffet – a staple of Indian restaurants in town, but only the Taj Pavilion seems to get it right.

Italian

Assaggi

1 Sanlitun Beixiaojie; tel: 8454 4508; daily 11.30am–2.30pm, 6–11.30pm; $$

Italian food served in an elegant setting; the glassed-in rooftop patio is particularly pleasant.

Mercante

4 Fangzhuanchang Hutong, Dongcheng; tel: 8402 5098; Mon–Fri 6pm–midnight, Sat–Sun noon–4pm, 6pm–midnight; $$

Finding such an authentic trattoria after wandering in the hutongs feels like a mirage. Yet in this rustic setting, Mercante's handmade pasta, fresh cheeses and excellent selection of wines could please even the pickiest Italian *nonna*. The relaxed atmosphere often translates to sluggish service, however, ensuring meals run late into the evening.

Japanese

Hatsune

Heqiao Dasha, 8A Guanghua Lu (east of the Kerry Centre), Chaoyang; tel: 6581 3939; 10.30am–2pm, 5.30–10pm; $$

This hip, sleek Japanese joint has a soundtrack and an inventive sushi menu to match. Here, things even Japanese people have never heard of are wrapped in seaweed. But almost everything is delicious. There are three restaurants featuring sushi, barbecue and hot pot.

Okra

Second Floor, Courtyard 4, 4 Gongti Beilu, Chaoyang; tel: 6593 5087; Tue–Sun 6–11pm; www.okra1949.com; $$$

Local celebrity chef Max Levy, formerly the only non-Japanese sushi chef at New York's Sushi Yasuda, has blown Beijing away with his idiosyncratic take on Japanese cuisine, sushi and seafood at Okra. His influence is present in not only the striking modern design and quirky soundtrack, but also in his imaginative flavour combinations made with extremely high quality fish and produce. Boutique sake and craft cocktails round out the reliably excellent meal.

Yotsuba

2 Xinyuan Zhongjie, Chaoyang; tel: 6464 2365; daily 11.30am–2pm, 5.30–10pm; www.yotsuba.com.cn; $$$

Yotsuba is a paradise for sushi lovers, with fish and seafood flown in from Tokyo's celebrated Tsukiji fish market but

Fine Chinese dining

at a fraction of a price you'd find there. The restaurant is only a couple of low-set tables and a sushi bar, making reservations necessary, but other branches have opened up around town.

Korean

One Pot

B1-238, Tower 2, Sanlitun SOHO, Gongti Beilu, Chaoyang; tel: 5935 9475; $$

The brainchild of Andrew Ahn, formerly of the W Hotel Seoul, this clinically-white Korean bistro pushes the limits of Korean street eats. Think cheese-stuffed rice cakes in pumpkin gravy, pear kimchi, and the most succulent roast chicken you can find in Beijing – the secret is an infusion of cherry beer.

Saveurs De Coree

20 Ju'er Hutong, Dongcheng; tel: 6401 6083; daily 11.30am–10.30pm; www.saveursdecoree.com.cn; $$

This lovely Korean bistro is hidden behind a glass-and-bamboo façade in the hutongs. While most of the city's Korean eateries offer barbecue and little else, you will be able to find more traditional offerings here, from noodles to delicately prepared beef and pork dishes. Stick around after your meal for a creative tipple at the associated soju bar.

Middle Eastern

Biteapitta

2/F, Tongli Studio, Sanlitun Houjie, Chaoyang; tel: 6467 2961; $

Simple Israeli eats like falafel, hummus and shawarma. The canteen-esque setting right on the bar street is uninspiring, though superior to all of its neighbours for a quick lunch or snack.

Muslim (Hui)

Kaorouji

14 Qianhai Dongyan, Lake District; tel: 6404 2554; daily 11am–2pm and 5–11pm; $$

Located in the Shichahai area, this is an old favourite with Beijing's Hui community, opened in 1848. It specialises in lamb, prepared in all manner – grilled, roasted or braised. The caged mynah birds that greet diners in Mandarin are a hit with children. Staff can arrange a meal on a boat on the nearby Qianhai Lake.

Russian

Traktirr

5–15 Dongzhimennei Dajie; tel: 8407 8158; daily 10am–10pm; $

Great Russian favourites are served here in a ski-chalet-esque atmosphere. Chicken Kiev is perennially popular, as are various dishes with mushroom and cream sauce, and borscht. If the original location is packed – and it often is – head out to Dongzhimennei Dajie and turn left for its second location.

Spanish

Niajo

Third Floor, Nali Patio, Chaoyang district; tel: 5208 6052; daily noon–11pm; $$

Sweet potato-noodles

Just like a good Spanish feast, there's a little bit of everything Iberian here. Though the trademark paella undoubtedly steals the show, there is a wide selection of tapas, Iberian ham and other Valencian treats as well. A good value lunch deal that changes weekly. The colourful décor, inspired by Gaudí, is a conversation starter.

Shanghainese/Nanjing
Nanjing Impressions
4/F, Shimao Department Store, 13 Gongti Beilu, Chaoyang; tel: 8405 9777; Mon-Fri 11am–2pm, 5–9.30pm, Sat–Sun 11am–10pm; $

Nanjing Impressions certainly lives up to its name, from the swaying red lanterns to the costumed waiters and occasional traditional music performances. The food is a faithful recreation of the small eats and snacks that are typical of the southern capital. Be sure to order the great duck specialties, like duck buns or salted duck.

Shanxi
Noodle Loft (Mianku)
Wangjing Lu, 33 Guangshunjie, Chaoyang district; tel: 6774 9950; daily 10am–10pm; $$

In this stylishly retro-cool environment with a noodle bar, slurp noodles of every kind and also enjoy other delicious specialties from Shanxi province. Watching the skilled chefs pull, shave, snip and shape noodles by hand before your eyes is almost as fun as eating them.

Sichuan
Chuan Ban
5 Gongyuan Toutiao, Dongcheng district; tel: 6512 2277 ext. 6101; Mon–Fri 11am–2pm, 5–9.30pm; Sat–Sun 11am–9.30pm; $$

Chuan Ban is often lauded as the most authentic place for Sichuanese food in Beijing, which is to be expected from the official restaurant of Sichuan province. The humbly decorated establishment serves textbook renditions of Sichuanese staples in a jovial, unrestrained atmosphere. Expect a (long) wait for a table.

Fei Teng Yu Xiang
Various locations, including: 36 Xingfu Yicun Sixiang (northern end of the car park opposite the Workers' Stadium), tel: 6417 4988; 1/F, Yehuayue Building, near the south gate of Scitech, tel: 6515 9600; daily 11am–2.30pm and 4.30–10.30pm; $

Chain restaurant featuring *shuizhu yu*, chunks of fish in a huge bowl of peppers and chilli sauce. These restaurants have much more extensive menus than other Sichuan spots and serve an enormous range of specialities that are hard to get elsewhere. The pork ribs, and anything with broccoli, are recommended.

South Beauty
Various locations, including: Pacific Century Place, Gongren Tiyuchang Beilu, tel: 6539 3502; China World Trade Centre, tel: 6505 0809; Oriental Plaza, tel: 8518 6971; Kerry

A typical Beijing restaurant

Fried fish with green peppers

Centre, tel: 8529 9458; daily 11am–11pm; $–$$

This upscale chain is representative of a new emphasis on dining style – the leather sofas and glass installations are just as responsible for its popularity as the Sichuan water-boiled fish and beef cooked on hot stones. It's popular with the business crowd for lunch and dinner.

Transit

N4-36, Taikoo Li North, Chaoyang; 6417 9090; daily 6–11pm; $$$

One of Beijing's most stylish Chinese restaurants, Transit elevates chilli-laden Sichuanese cuisine through innovative combinations, less oil and breathlessly elegant preparation. Dishes like dan dan noodles and koushuiji mouthwatering chicken are well-suited to the dim, designer setting of contemporary art and attentive service. It's attached to an equally flashy ultralounge next door, which can provide specialist cocktails. Prices are high, so bring your expense card if you have one.

Xiheyaju

North-eastern corner of Ritan Park, Chaoyang; tel: 8561 7643; daily 11am–2.30pm and 5–10pm; $$

Other than Sichuan food, this restaurant, popular with tourists and expats, serves up a range of other regional Chinese cuisines, including Cantonese, Shanghainese and north-eastern. Enjoy your meal in the pretty courtyard.

Southeast Asian

Lau Pa Sak

North-western corner of the intersection of Xindong Lu and Dongzhimenwai Dajie, opposite the Canadian Embassy, Chaoyang; tel: 6417 0952; daily 11am–11pm; $

Southeast Asian noodle, rice and curry dishes, with a smattering of dishes inspired by Singaporean street food. Sambal-flavoured everything is delicious, as is the dry *beef rendang* curry (good luck finishing it) and seafood stews that smell enchantingly of sea mud. The sweet coffee and curry puffs are must-tries.

My Humble House

L2-12, Parkview Green, 9 Dongdaqiao Lu, Chaoyang; tel: 8518 8811; daily 11.30am–2.30pm, 5.30–10pm; www.myhumble house.com.sg; $$$

Forget the self-congratulatory name: set in an airy, glass-walled dining room flanked by lush bamboo, this upscale Singaporean restaurant treats its food as if it were a refined work of art. The restaurant blends Chinese culinary traditions with global influences, leading to delicious renditions of Peranakan laksa and even Peking duck with photo-perfect presentations. The lunch menu is good value.

Pak Pak

1/F, Bldg AB, Guanghua International, 10 Jintong Xilu, Chaoyang; tel: 8590 6956; daily 10am–10pm; $$

Exceptional Thai in a business-casual atmosphere of pressed glass and

A Beijing feast

bamboo, located right in the CBD. Portions are large and spices are strong, expressed in some interesting dishes like curry mashed potatoes along well-done conventional noodles and soups. Don't skip out on the top-notch desserts, either.

Tex-Mex
The Taco Bar
1/F, Unit 10, Courtyard 4, Nansanlitun Lu, Chaoyang; tel: 6501 6026; www.tacobar china.com; $

The perpetually popular Taco Bar is a veritable institution for the hipper members of the Beijing expat community, who rave about the winning tacos, massive salads and indie-chic setting.

Tibetan
Makye Ame
11A Xiushui Nanjie, behind Friendship Store, Chaoyang; tel: 6506 9616; daily 11.30am–2am; $

Authentic food, comfy couches and a cosy atmosphere, until the nightly song-and-dance show, which treads the line between cheese and fascination. Real Tibetan food may consist largely of yak, yak by-products and barley, but Makye Ame has made a brave attempt to turn survival food into a cuisine. Try the goat and yoghurt dishes as well as the yak.

Vegetarian
Bodhi-Sake
16 Heiyaochang Jie, Xicheng; tel: 6355 7348; daily 10am–11pm; $$

Tucked inside the courtyard of a Buddhist temple in southern Beijing, this little eatery is run by its monks. Vegetarian cuisine is served in a tranquil atmosphere marked by chanting and religious music. As in most Buddhist restaurants in Beijing, 'mock meat', made from tofu, nuts and other vegetable proteins, is a main feature. The sausages, beef and fish, are nearly indistinguishable from the real thing.

Gongdelin
158 Qianmen Nandajie, Qianmen; tel: 6702 0867; daily 10.30am–8.30pm; $

This Buddhist vegetarian restaurant, opened in 1922, is an excellent choice despite the nondescript decor and lacklustre service. Order 'mock meat' dishes, crafted from tofu, mushrooms and vegetables, from its English menu.

Pure Lotus Vegetarian
10 Nongzhan Nanli, Chaoyang Park; tel: 6592 3627; daily 11am–11pm; $$$

Probably the highest-regarded vegetarian restaurant in town, the food may cost the earth but it is certainly heavenly. Tofu, grains and special spices make the fake meat good enough to convert die-hard carnivores.

Vietnamese
Nuage
22 Qianhai Lake East Bank; tel: 6401 9581; daily 11am–1pm; $$

Greens with shredded chicken

This Vietnamese restaurant's languid style and lakeside location give it the sultry atmosphere of a tropical escape. The view over the back lacks and Drum Tower from the terrace is worth the 15 percent service charge.

Susu

10 Qianliang Hutong Xi Xiang, Dongcheng; tel: 8400 2699; Tue–Sun 11am–11pm; www.susubeijing.com; $$

Few hutong spots give such a stunning first impression as Susu, a restored courtyard that houses one of the city's finest Vietnamese restaurants. The restaurant's subtle lighting gently accents the understated setting, making it a romantic spot with a uniquely Beijing atmosphere. The Vietnamese fare is just as memorable, with great DIY spring rolls, claypot dishes and warming bowls of pho.

Xinjiang

Xinjiang Islam Restaurant

Xinjiang Provincial Government Office, 7 Sanlihe Lu, Xicheng district; tel: 6830 1820; daily 11am–10.30pm; $

The Xinjiang Government's official restaurant is a loud, proud celebration of tender lamb and hearty noodles. Don't miss the house-made yoghurt.

Xinjiang Red Rose

7 Xingfu Yicun, opposite the Workers' Stadium North Gate; tel: 6415 5741; daily 11am–11pm; $$

Hookah pipes, nightly music, Uighur dancing girls and excellent *dapanji* ('big plate chicken'). Large groups can get rather boisterous.

Yunnanese

Dali Courtyard

67 Xiaojingchang Hutong, Gulou Dongdajie; tel: 8404 1430; daily 11am–2pm, 6–11pm; $$

Set in a beautiful courtyard, this popular restaurant offers a set menu only according to what the chefs are prepared to cook on a given day.

Golden Peacock

16 Minzu Daxue Beilu, Weigongcun, Haidian; tel: 6893 2030; daily 11am–9pm; $

Ethnic minority cuisine is often most authentic in the vicinity of the Central University for Nationalities, and the Golden Peacock, serving the food of the Dai minority, is exceptional. The waitstaff are all from Yunnan, as are the regional delicacies such as fried potato balls, sticky rice in half a pineapple, and fish done fifty different ways.

In and Out

1 Sanlitun Beixiaojie, Chaoyang; tel: 8454 0086; 11am–10pm daily; $

This three-level, Lijiang-themed eatery is well-regarded among both expats and locals for its jumble of minority cuisine standards. The costumed waiters fit in perfectly, as does the fried goat cheese, fish roasted with lemongrass and over-the-bridge noodles.

NIGHTLIFE

Chaoyang and CBD

BBC

1 Taipingzhuang Nanli, Chaoyang (across from The Big Smoke); no tel

Crammed into a tiny space with no sign outside, BBC feels more like climbing into a deluxe alcohol cabinet than a bar. Each cocktail is bespoke; just tell the bartender what you're into, and he shakes something up using top-shelf spirits and homemade bitters. Some might complain the setting feels affected, with wax-seal receipts and optional straight razor shaves (really), but cocktail aficionados will adore it.

Blue Frog

Third floor, Building 4, Sanlitun Village; tel: 6417 4030

Though more famous for its hamburgers, Blue Frog is also a place Sanlitun Village's shoppers are grateful for thanks to its quality liquid refreshments. The rooftop and well-trained staff are a bonus.

Centro

Lobby, Kerry Centre, 1 Guanghua Lu; tel: 6561 8833/42

The Kerry Centre aimed to make Centro the poshest lounge in town, and to a large extent it has succeeded. From the decor to the performing bartenders, everything about Centro could easily stray over the top, but as a whole it still manages to stay classy. Jazz acts imported from the US play nightly, international businessmen relax after a day of deal-making, and London-priced cocktails are half-price before 6pm.

Destination

Opposite Workers' Stadium West Gate; tel: 6551 5138

By far the city's largest dedicated gay bar with a clientele that is 90 percent male. Destination is a popular spot for dancing and cruising that sometimes hosts community events.

Drei Kronen 1308

5 China View, Workers' Stadium East Road; tel: 6503 5555

A counterintuitively large microbrewery serving wallet-lightening but excellent steins of pilsner, wheat beer and dark beer. Staff manage to be friendly despite being decked out in clichéd German costume: think lederhosen or braided pigtails.

Fubar

Inside Workers' Stadium East Gate; tel: 6593 8227

A speakeasy themed cocktail bar tucked away behind a hidden door at the back of a hot dog stall may sound like a gimmick too far, even after they've put a sign outside to advertise the cav-

Low-lit drinking in Houhai

ernous space. Rarely seen bottles such as Maker's Mark and Green Chartreuse sit proudly behind the bar.

Janes and Hooch

4 Gongti Beilu, Across from The Rug, Chaoyang; tel: 6403 2757; www.janesand hooch.com

This modern reimagining of a prohibition-era speakeasy has taken home several local and international 'best-of' awards. Socialite types frequent here for the outstanding, if extortionately priced, cocktails, as well as the intimate, jazz-age flair.

Jing-A (京A) Brewing

Building B, 1949 The Hidden City, Courtyard 4, Gongti Beilu, Chaoyang; tel:6501 8883; www.capitalbrew.com

A noticeable newcomer on the Beijing craft brewery map, Jing-A offers playful offerings like watermelon wheat alongside their very good brews. Gourmet food options like Gouda grilled cheese, beer-battered fish and chips and sweet potato fries round out the menu.

LAN Club

4/F LG Twin Towers, B12 Jianguomenwai Dajie; tel 5109 6012

A glamorous, Philippe Starck-designed interior makes this one of Beijing's most eye-catching venues. LAN Club boasts an impressive wine cellar and cigar lounge but also courts the younger crowd with themed parties.

The Local

Courtyard 4 (across the parking lot of 1949 the Hidden City), Gongti Beilu, Chaoyang; tel: 6591 5925; www.beijing-local.com

Enormous television screens spread over two floors and multiple satellite feeds make The Local a good choice to catch a game of any type. They offer a bargain daily happy hour, which is a good way to take advantage of the wide selection of craft brew, imported Belgian beer and big portions of quality bar food.

Migas

6/F, 81 Sanlitun Lu, Chaoyang; tel: 5208 6061; www.migasbj.com

Migas is hands-down Beijing's best rooftop bar. Somehow, the roof of an excellent modern Spanish restaurant became where Beijing's most fashionable go to be on the scene, dancing to funk or techno or lounging with a large cocktail. There is a smaller indoor bar downstairs for when it's too cold. Cover charge.

Paddy O'Sheas

28 Dongzhimenwai Dajie, Sanlitun; tel: 6415 6389

An Irish pub popular for draught Guinness, reasonably priced drinks and standard bar food. Televised sports matches and pool/darts upstairs make this a popular spot for sports fans.

The Tree

43 Sanlitun Beijie, behind Poachers Inn; tel: 6415 1954

Tucked round the corner away from Sanlitun's less sophisticated bars, the Tree's cosy pub atmosphere makes it a perennial favourite. Belgian beers and an authentic pizza oven ensure this is one of Sanlitun's best spots for lunch or an evening's entertainment.

Vics
Inside Workers' Stadium North Gate; tel: 5293 0333

Vics is the largest nightclub in the Workers' Stadium north gate section and for all its faults keeps the crowds happy and remains popular year after year. Expect crowds of fashionable young people and loud hip-hop music.

Chaoyang Park

Mokihi
Third Floor, C12 Haoyun Jie; tel: 5867 0244

A Japanese cocktail bar (next to Edomae Sushi, look out for the sign) that justifies high prices with precisionmade cocktails including the implausible wasabi martini and wonderful Earl Grey MarTEAni. A classic-styled bar and jazz music make this a hard place to leave.

The World of Suzie Wong
1A Nongzhanguan Lu; tel: 6500 3377

This three-floored opium-den styled nightclub is responsible for kick-starting the whole Chaoyang Park-area nightlife scene. The occasional celebrity visitor and a female clientele who clearly put more effort into looking glamorous than enjoying their drinks

will make this Beijing mainstay too pretentious for some.

Lake District

Amilal
48 Shoubi Hutong, Dongcheng; tel: 8404 1416

A simple courtyard with outsize character: the antique furniture, living-room feel and good selection of imported beers and whiskeys make this hutong hideaway stand out. The owner puts his own photography up on display as well as other local artworks.

Capital Spirits
3 Daju Hutong, Dongcheng; tel: 6409 3319

Most non-Chinese can't stand the taste of local firewater baijiu, but Capital Spirits gives adventurous drinkers a reason to change their minds. Order a flight of thimble-sized shots, and the waitstaff will explain the nuances and flavour profiles of each type. If you really can't stand the taste, original cocktails, house-distilled spirits and exotic beers are also on offer.

Dada
206 Gulou Dongdajie, tel: 183 1108 0818

Strong drinks, blasting beats and an industrial underground vibe keep Beijing's hip set dancing here until dawn. DJs spin alternative or experimental electronic music almost every night of the week, though keep in mind the parties start and end late. No charge most nights.

East Shore Live Jazz Café
2 Shichahai Nanyan, Xicheng; tel: 8403 2131

Lotus Lane Bar Strip

Established by Chinese rock legend Cui Jian's saxophonist, this enduring fixture on the music circuit has good live jazz music Wednesday to Sunday nights (from 10pm). The relaxed atmosphere, with bay windows looking out at the lights over Qianhai Lake, more than makes up for the underwhelming drinks. No cover charge.

El Nido
59 Fangjia Hutong; tel: 8402 9495
The exceedingly simple concept of this hutong dive assures its lasting popularity. Grab one of the imported bottled beers from the fridge yourself, give some cash to the attendant and take a seat on one of the benches. The dirt-cheap prices, copious outdoor seating and anything-goes feel attracts a motley crew of regulars, and you're bound to hear some interesting stories if you talk them up.

Modernista
44 Baochao Hutong, Dongcheng
Modernista's belle époque theme is done so well it could be down a Parisian back alley. Checkerboard floors, copious absinthe and cheap imported beers and cocktails attract a lively crowd, which packs out the bar during the frequent swing dancing classes, burlesque shows and art nights.

Siif
67 Beiluoguxiang, Dongcheng; tel: 6406 9496
The long, bustling *hutong* Nanluogu Xiang can hardly be considered off the beaten path any longer. Hidden in nearby Beiluoguxiang, Siif is definitely worth hunting out for cheap drinks and a relaxed crowd. There's a simple balcony and even simpler basement dance floor.

Tao Yao Bar
Beiguanfang Hutong, (300m/yds west of Silver Ingot Bridge); tel: 8322 8585
This Tibetan-themed bar carves itself a nice little niche out of the area's mishmash of nightlife. Milk tea, of course, and beers are served up just far enough away from the throngs of Houhai tourists to create a peaceful spot.

Yugong Yishan
3 Zhangxizhong Lu, Dongcheng; tel: 6404 2711
Yugong Yishan is by far Beijing's best-known live music venue. Their sound system is decent and the management just professional enough to regularly attract foreign talent. Grungy locals grudgingly stump up full prices for drinks and the occasional pop or rock star can be seen at the bar.

Western suburbs

The Garden Bar and Terrace
Shangri-La Hotel, 29 Zizhuyuan Lu; tel: 6841 2211
The ideal spot for drinks after a visit to the Summer Palace, this wine bar's garden impresses with a marble bridge over a tree-shaded stream, lazy Koi carp and a decent selection of wine at reasonable prices.

Signage at a foreign bank

A–Z

A

Age restrictions

Age restrictions for various venues and activities are lax or non-existent. Laws that ban minors from internet cafés, for example, may exist, but they are rarely enforced. It is also not uncommon to see young children purchasing alcohol or cigarettes, presumably for their parents. At the most, some rides in amusement parks may refuse very small children, and venue ticket prices are often graded according to age.

Airline offices

The majority of foreign airline offices can be found in and around the Yansha Friendship Shopping Mall, on the northeast Dongsanhuan Lu (Third Ring Road). Try www.thebeijinger.com or www.timeoutbeijing.com for an up-to-date list of addresses and phone numbers.

China's national tourist offices and travel agencies, including hotel travel desks, can give you the current flight schedule of domestic airlines. You can buy tickets from travel agencies or airline booking offices. Travel agencies may be more convenient, and are more likely to have English-speaking staff, although they are likely to charge more. Ticket offices around town sell air tickets, look out for pictures of trains and planes on the signage of small shops. Otherwise, try **China International Travel Services** (CITS; tel: 400 600 8888; www.cits.com.cn)

B

Budgeting

For many aspects of travel, particularly food and transport, it will be significantly cheaper in China than Western countries. Beijing is trying hard to play catch-up, however, and you may be occasionally surprised by high prices.

Accommodation can cost anywhere from 50 yuan for dormitory beds in youth hostels to luxury prices for rooms in international hotels. An average double room in a hotel will cost from 350 to 600 yuan per night. Dining expenses can likewise vary; in a typical Chinese restaurant you will end up spending 50 to 100 yuan per person. A bus ride is usually 1 yuan and a trip on the subway is 2 yuan, while taxi fares start at 10 yuan and may reach 30 yuan for a longer trip within the city. Admission tickets start from a few yuan for an average park to 60 yuan for the Forbidden City. Most large museums and exhibitions charge 35 to 50 yuan.

Beijing police

Business hours

Business hours vary. Government offices, including banks, are generally open 8am–5pm. Some close earlier and most have a lunch break from noon to 1pm. Offices also open on Saturday mornings, but not on Sundays. The best time to get things done is at the start of the working day – many government offices are reluctant to do anything after 3pm.

Most shops open at 9am and close around 9pm, though if they are still state-run they may close by 6pm. Many department stores and privately run small stores open until 9pm. Money exchange outlets – but not banks – are open seven days a week and also generally operate long hours. At tourist sights, ticket sales may stop 30 minutes before closing time and many museums are closed on Mondays.

Children

Those travelling with children should take care out in the streets, as Beijing's traffic is notoriously chaotic and unpredictable. Illness can be an issue, as well: people from all over China and the world congregate in Beijing, bringing their colds with them, and each season presents its unique health risks, not helped by the poor air quality. Information and advice on almost every child-related concern imaginable is available on Beijing Kids (www.beijing-kids.com).

Climate

The best time to visit Beijing is from early September through to late November, when it is normally dry and sunny, with moderate temperatures. If you visit between March and May, chances are you will encounter at least one of the annual dust storms that blow in from the Gobi Desert. Summers are hot and muggy, with occasional torrential downpours. The temperature in the hottest month, July, averages 30°C (86°F) but it can occasionally soar to nearly 40°C (104°F). Beijing winters are cold and very dry but mostly sunny. The coldest month, January, averages about -5°C (23°F), but temperatures can drop to as low as -23°C (-9°F). It generally snows once or twice during the winter, and spring may see three or four monsoon-type downpours. Otherwise, there is little precipitation. A polluted haze is the norm for Beijing skies apart from during summer months. During holidays and important events, cloud seeding is often used to help produce glorious weather.

Clothing

Shorts, sandals and a sun hat are necessary in summer, while winter calls for heavy coats and warm hats. Locals wear several layers of clothing all win-

ter. One of the best buys in Beijing is silk thermal underwear. Beijing is a great city to explore on foot, so comfortable walking shoes are essential. Remember to have something waterproof (or at least an umbrella) with you in spring or autumn, as showers are quite common.

Crime and safety

Violent crime is very rare in Beijing, at least when it comes to foreigners. Walking the streets at night is quite safe, and there are no 'bad' parts of town. Women, even those travelling alone, can expect to go unharassed. That said, pickpockets are a danger in most public places. When in crowded areas, keep an eye on wallets and other valuables, and never leave belongings unattended. Scams are the most common risk and the teahouse con remains popular around Wangfujing and Tiananmen: friendly locals approach out-of-towners to invite them to a teahouse but don't pick up the extortionate bill. Taxi drivers should always use the meter. The police are willing to receive reports and do what they can to help, but only rarely can they actually retrieve stolen items.

Customs

Written declarations are required only of visitors carrying more than US$5,000 or who exceed duty-free limits. Chinese customs are especially sensitive to pornographic material as well as publications deemed to be anti-government, which can be a surprisingly wide category. Foreign visitors are also advised not to bring more than one copy of the Bible into China. Antiques dating from prior to 1795 cannot be legally taken out of the country. Foreigners carrying illicit drugs have been sentenced to long prison terms. Take care when bringing DVDs or CDs out of the country – Chinese customs will let them pass, but customs in your home country may not.

D

Disabled travellers

Beijing is woefully unprepared for disabled travellers: textured paths on the sidewalks, ostensibly for the blind, are the sole concession to the disabled. Wheelchair ramps are very slowly catching on, but they are in so few locations that it makes little difference. Public transport is entirely inaccessible to wheelchairs; even those on crutches will have difficulties.

E

Electricity

Electrical current runs at 220 volts. Many hotels have 110-volt shaver sockets. Most outlets can accept both parallel- and angled-prong plugs.

Embassies

Embassies are generally located either in the Jianguomen area, Sanlitun or Ritan Park locale.

Chinese flag

Australia: 21 Dongzhimenwai Dajie; tel: 5140 4111
Canada: 19 Dongzhimenwai Dajie; tel: 5139 4448
Ireland: 3 Ritan Lu, Jianguomen; tel: 6532 2691
UK: 11 Guanghua Lu, Jianguomenwai; tel: 5192 4000
US: 55 Anjialou Lu, Chaoyang District; tel: 8531 3000

Emergencies

All emergency hotlines provide English-language service.
Ambulance: 120 for service
Fire: 119
Police: 110
Traffic accidents: 122
International SOS: 6590 3419
Beijing tourist complaint hotline: 12301

Etiquette

Chinese society is famous for its complex rules of propriety and etiquette, and it will be difficult for the casual visitor to master them. Luckily most Chinese will make considerable allowances for foreign guests, and a healthy dose of enthusiasm and friendliness will be enough for you to get by. In general, one can never be too modest or appreciative of others' good qualities. Refuse gifts before accepting them (and expect to be refused at first), offer to pay for everything, and try to anticipate others' needs. The 'please-and-thank-you' style of Western courtesy doesn't count for much – you should make an effort to *do* something to express gratitude, even if everyone knows that it is just a show. When eating or drinking together, it is considered very rude to split the bill, and if asking someone out for a meal it is customary for the host to pay for everything.

Faux pas generally involves embarrassing friends or acquaintances in some way or a lack of necessary flattery. Let mistakes and inconveniences go by, if possible, or if not, bring them up as gently as you can. Avoid putting people on the spot unexpectedly, and, of course, topics of diplomatic sensitivity, such as the sovereignty, Tibet or Taiwan, should be avoided unless someone else brings them up first.

As anywhere, when visiting Buddhist temples dress conservatively – no bare legs or shoulders. Young Chinese follow global fashions, but while girls may wear short skirts and shorts in the summer, cleavage is rarely on show.

Festivals

The three main holidays in China (the three 'Golden Weeks') are Spring Festival (January/February), May First, and October First (China's National Day). Each holiday occasions a week off work, and the entire country more or less grinds to a halt. These are

Inside a traditional Chinese pharmacy

absolutely awful times to travel, as the whole nation tries to take the train all at once, and most businesses close for the week. If you are here for one of these periods, don't plan on getting around much. The government has been considering abolishing the weeklong holidays and spreading the days off around the calendar, a move many consider wise and long overdue.

Other important traditional holidays include the Lantern Festival in late February/early March, Tomb Sweeping Day at the beginning of April, and Mid Autumn Day (Moon Festival) in late September/early October.

Gay and lesbian travellers

Homosexuality is still an awkward subject in China. It was only removed from the list of mental disorders in 2001, and social acceptance has been slow in coming. As Chinese generally dislike public confrontation, homosexual people are rarely harassed openly, but gay pride events are still regularly shut down by the police. The flipside of this is that the underground gay scene is thriving. For English-language nightlife information try www.utopia-asia.com.

Government

Beijing is the capital of the People's Republic of China. Xi Jinping is the general secretary of the Communist Party of China (CPC), president of the country, and the chairman of the CPC-controlled Military Commission. Li Keqiang is the premier. The 3,000-strong legislative body, the National People's Congress (NPC) meets annually in Beijing. In theory, the NPC can approve or reject legislation, but it is widely regarded as a rubber-stamp parliament. Real power lies with the nine members of the Standing Committee of the CPC Politburo (also known as China's cabinet). Most government bodies have a corresponding body in the party structure, and it is usually the party that wields actual authority. Personal connections and bureaucracy remain key features of day-to-day government and civil service operations.

Beijing is one of the four municipalities with status equal to that of China's provinces, along with Shanghai, Tianjin and Chongqing. It is divided into 12 separate administrative districts. The city's local government set-up mirrors that of the central government; it is led by the Communist Party with limited participation by non-party officials.

The economy is in transition from socialism to a 'socialist market economy'. The capital is still behind many southern and coastal cities in encouraging capitalism. Hence, institutions such as banks and post offices are still caught in the grip of the old system, but the new system is evident in the huge number of privately run restaurants and retail outlets.

Street newspaper vendor

H

Health

Tap water should always be boiled before it is drunk. Some hotels have water purification systems and all sell bottled water and provide flasks of boiled water in guest rooms. Brushing teeth with tap water is not a problem. Bottled water and canned soft drinks are available at tourist sights and sold on most streets.

Although they are not necessarily unsafe, avoid ice cream, yoghurt and drinks from large vats. If buying food from street vendors, make sure it is piping hot and freshly cooked and served in clean dishes, preferably disposable ones. Don't patronise restaurants with dirty utensils or poor food-handling practices, to avoid contracting hepatitis, which is endemic. Wash your hands frequently, and peel or wash fruit. Except in hotels, most toilets are the crude, though renovated, squat type. Carry your own toilet paper.

Colds and stomach disorders are the most common travellers' complaints. Attention to hygiene goes a long way towards preventing both. Medicines that may come in handy are paracetemol, a stomach 'stopper' like Lomotil/Imodium, a heartburn remedy and aspirin. Watsons, with outlets all over the city, has a wide selection of Western medicines.

Malaria prevention medication is not necessary for Beijing or anywhere in northern China.

Consult your doctor or a travel clinic nurse for recommended vaccinations (eg. Hepatitis A) before travelling to China. In the UK, MASTA (Medical Advisory Service for Travellers Abroad) can provide up-to-date information (tel: 0906 8 224 100) on all medical matters.

Medical Services: In case of dire emergency, dial 120 for an ambulance; or call the Beijing International SOS Clinic (5 Sanlitun Xiwujie; tel: 6462 9112; 24-hour alarm tel: 6462 9100).

Two of the best hospitals for foreigners are the **Sino-Japanese Friendship Hospital** (northern end of Heping Lu; tel: 6422 2952) and the **Peking Union Medical Hospital** (53 Dongdanbei Dajie; emergency tel: 6529 5284). The best place for treatment of serious illness is the private Beijing United Family Heath Centre (B1/F, St Regis Hotel, 21 Jianguomenwai Dajie, Chaoyang District; tel 8532 1221). All staff speak English.

Pharmacies: These are plentiful and usually open 24 hours. A wide variety of medicines are available, including some that might require a prescription in other countries. Staff often recommend the most expensive products, however, and some suggest remedies might seem positively bizarre to a westerner.

Chinese bank notes

I

Internet

Getting online is getting easier and easier in Beijing. Nearly every hotel in Beijing offers some sort of access, either wireless or broadband in the room, or computers in the lobby or business centre. Internet cafés are common and may be less expensive, though some might ask for your passport number before allowing you online. Free wireless internet in cafés and bars is almost ubiquitous. The 'Great Firewall' of Internet censorship is powerful, and Facebook, Twitter, YouTube, Google and other websites commonly used in the West are not accessible without a VPN (virtual private network).

L

Language

Large hotels usually have many English-speaking staff. Otherwise, you will find that most people speak only a little English. English, French, Japanese, Italian, German and Spanish interpreters can be hired through major hotels or CITS. Prices are negotiable depending on the group's size.

Left luggage and lost property

Lost property that is presumed stolen should be reported to the Foreigners Section of the **Beijing Public Security Bureau**, tel: 6525 5486. Beijing does not have a central lost-property office, but the **Beijing Tourist Hotline** (tel: 6513 0828) may provide some advice on where to seek help. Taxis are a common place to lose things, which is why it's always advisable to ask for a receipt – this will have the telephone number of the taxi company and your driver's identification number on it. For the airport lost and found, tel: 6459 8333.

M

Maps

A variety of street and tourist maps are available free from the CITS Information Centre at 27 Sanlitun Beilu (tel: 6417 6627). Reasonably accurate maps in English are available from most hotels. Bookshops and kiosks mainly sell Chinese maps, which usually include bus and subway routes. Some maps have street and building names in both Chinese characters and English. The *Insight Flexi Map to Beijing* is durable, detailed and easy to use, with a full street index, and its laminated finish means that getting it wet in a Beijing summer rainstorm is not a problem.

Media

Newspapers: The English-language *China Daily* reports domestic and foreign news with an official slant. *Global Times* (www.globaltimes.cn) is similar but in a tabloid format. For local list-

ings, pick up a copy of *Time Out Beijing* (www.timeoutbeijing.com) around town. *The International Herald Tribune, Asian Wall Street Journal* and international news magazines are available at 5-star hotels, though often a day late. The websites of the New York Times, Bloomberg News, and a few other outlets are unaccessible in the country.

Television: Most major hotels offer CNN's 24-hour programmes. Star TV from Hong Kong is also available. China Central Television broadcasts English-language news and programming on CCTV 9 while local and most imported programmes are broadcast in Chinese. Local radio broadcasts in English and other languages can be heard on 91.5FM and 87.5FM.

Money

Currency: The Chinese currency is the renminbi (RMB or 'people's currency') or yuan. Hotel rates are often cited in US dollars, but can be paid in yuan. Foreign currency can be exchanged in banks, the Friendship Store and some big shopping centres. A passport is usually required for any kind of money exchange.

When you change foreign currency into yuan, you get a receipt that allows you to change an equivalent sum of yuan back to foreign currency within six months. Be sure to keep all such receipts.

Chinese money is counted in yuan, jiao and fen. One yuan is 100 fen or 10 jiao; one jiao is 10 fen. Colloquially, a yuan is usually called a kuai and a jiao is called a mao. Bills are denominated in 1, 2 and 5 jiao, and 1, 2, 5, 10, 20, 50 and 100 yuan. There are also 1-yuan, 5-jiao and 1-jiao coins, plus 1-, 2- and 5-fen coins, which are almost worthless.

Credit Cards: Major credit and charge cards like Diner's Club, American Express, MasterCard, Visa and JCB are accepted at all but low-budget hotels. Some restaurants and stores geared toward tourists also accept them.

The most reliable place to cash travellers' cheques is at the Bank of China. Hotels catering to foreigners as well as large branches of other major banks are also able to handle them.

ATMs: Using credit cards to withdraw cash from ATMs is generally practicable, though a bit hit-and-miss. In general, machines marked with Cirrus, Plus, Star, Visa or MasterCard, can be used for withdrawing cash, though there are regular 'network errors'. Outside the airport, the most reliable bank in the city is the Bank of China at the southern end of Wangfujing, followed by the one in the basement of the World Trade Centre. Beyond that, the bigger the bank, the better luck you will have. Always withdraw cash in advance, and never leave yourself dependent on a particular withdrawal succeeding.

Money changers: Since Chinese yuan is not fully convertible to foreign cur-

rency, there is a small black market for foreign currency.

The main reason why the black market still persists is that it is technically illegal for most Chinese businesses to conduct foreign currency transactions, so they obtain foreign currency through illegal channels. If you must change money on the black market, avoid money changers who try to rush you, who ask you to walk into a back-street with them, or who are not obviously connected with a store. These people are often very good at sleight of hand. The 'safest' places to change money illegally are in the stores and market stalls.

Price differences: In 1996, China officially abolished the practice of charging foreigners higher prices for hotels, entrance to tourist sights and so on. Most places have complied, resulting in large price rises for Chinese visitors. But vendors at markets, food stands and privately run restaurants often try to charge foreigners more, as in many countries. The best way to deal with this is to find out local prices as soon as possible and insist on paying them, or walk away. If you are unsure of prices in a restaurant, find out the prices of individual dishes before ordering them.

Tipping: In Chairman Mao's time, tipping was thought of as a bourgeois affectation. These days, some hotel staff have come to expect tips, especially restroom attendants and bell boys. Taxi drivers and door attendants do not expect tips. Restaurants catering to foreigners usually add a 10 or 15 percent service charge to the bill, which goes straight to the owners, and waiters will almost never accept tips.

Overcharging and fake money: Overcharging in shops and taxis often happens, as does receiving counterfeit bills (usually 100s and 50s, though sometimes 20s as well) as change. In general, it is a good idea to know what things cost ahead of time, and ask that salespeople replace suspect currency.

Photography

Digital and film photography are both relatively convenient in Beijing. Film is readily available, and film development can be done at Kodak chain stores around the city, usually costing 30 yuan or so, plus another 10 or 15 if you want to scan the negatives. Processing for digital photography is also widely available – most photo shops will be able to read memory cards and download photos into discs, or make photographic prints from discs and memory cards.

Postal services

Mail: Hotel desks provide the most convenient service for posting letters and parcels. The International Post Office (tel: 6512 8120; 8am–6.30pm)

Tour group at the Great Wall

on Yabao Lu, about 300m/yds north of the Jianguomen junction, handles international mail and is Beijing's poste restante address.

Courier Services: International express courier services in Beijing include DHL (tel: 6466 5566), FedEx (tel: 6468 5566), TNT (tel: 800-810 9868) and UPS (tel: 6530 1234).

Public holidays

The following are official non-working days in China. The official list is not released until the December of the previous year. They may combine with a weekend to provide a longer break.

1 January: New Year's Day
January/February: Spring Festival (a 3-day minimum, dates vary according to the lunar calendar)
8 March: International Women's Day (half-day for women only)
April: Tomb Sweeping Day (1 day, usually April 4 or 5)
1 May: International Workers' Day (5 days)
June: Dragon Boat Festival (1 day, according to lunar calendar)
September: Mid Autumn Festival (1 day, according to lunar calendar)
1 October: National Day (5 days).

R

Religion

For most of the period of Communist rule since 1949, worship of all kinds was discouraged or actively sup-

pressed. Since 1978, the main religions have been allowed to revive, although many urban Chinese are atheists. Buddhism, Taoism, Islam and Christianity are all practised in temples, mosques and churches around Beijing.

Evangelising outside these institutions is forbidden and all religious groups are supposed to register with the government. Even so, Beijing has some underground (i.e. unregistered) Christian groups, particularly Catholic groups loyal to the Pope, which are technically illegal in China.

English language services are held at only a few churches, including the Catholic Nantang Cathedral, 141 Qianmen Dajie tel: 6602 6538 (right outside Xuanwumen subway station), and Protestant Chongwenmen Church, 2 Hougou Hutong, Chongwenmennei (tel: 6513 3549).

Smoking

A nationwide indoor smoking ban at public venues was introduced in 2011 though many, if not most, bars and restaurants are reticent to displease customers by enforcing it. On public transport, smokers will usually stop smoking immediately if asked.

Sport

All large hotels have sports facilities including gymnasia, tennis courts and

swimming pools, which are available to guests at no charge; many also allow non-guests to use these facilities for a fee. There are also a number of private gyms in Beijing, including the international chains **Clark Hatch** (tel: 6466-288) and **Bally Fitness** (Basement Level, Chang An Theatre; tel: 6518-1666), some of which offer daily or weekly rates for non-members.

A number of Olympic venues are open to the public for sports activities. The **National Aquatics Centre** (www.water-cube.com), for instance has several swimming pools and a water park. **The National Olympic Sports Centre** (www.bjnosc.com) has a wide range of facilities including tennis and basketball.

T

Telephones

Calls (land line) within Beijing are generally free. In most hotels you can telephone abroad direct, though this is expensive and in some you still need to ask the operator to call for you. In top hotels, you can use credit cards and international telephone cards. China's IDD rates have fallen but are still higher than most Western countries; remember that costs are halved after 6pm and at weekends.

Payphones which accept phonecards can be found along most city streets and in many hotels and shop-ping centres. These 'IC' cards (30, 50 or 100 yuan) can be bought at streetside newspaper kiosks or small shops, as well as from hotels. Small shops also sell prepaid internet phonecards called 'IP' cards, which offer considerably lower rates than standard costs and can in theory be used from any phone – before dialling the number you wish to reach, you need to dial a local number printed on the card followed by a PIN number. US credit-phonecard codes from China can be accessed by dialling 108 7901.

The International Post Office on the Second Ring Road north of the Jianguomen intersection (8am – 7pm) handles long-distance calls and money orders. The Long-Distance Telephone Building at Fuxingmen Dajie (7am–midnight) handles long-distance, conference and pre-booked calls.

Local calls can still be made from roadside booths with attendants, although as cellphones become ever more commonplace, these are disappearing. They generally cost four jiao. These booths can also be used for long-distance calls but charges can be high.

Dial 115 for operator assistance with long-distance calls, and 114 for directory enquiries. The country code for China is 86, and the area code for Beijing is 10, which does not need to be dialled for calls within the city and is not included in the Beijing phone numbers listed in this guidebook.

Luggage collection at the airport

Time differences

Beijing time is eight hours ahead of Greenwich Mean Time (GMT), and there is no daylight-saving time. The entire country follows Beijing's time zone, even at its western extremities.

Toilets

Public toilets are readily available in Beijing, but that does not mean you are going to like them. Conditions vary wildly, from filthy concrete set-ups in the *hutongs* to plush facilities in larger hotels. New chemical toilets are popping up around town, and while they are a step in the right direction, there is still a long way to go. If you learn no other Chinese characters, you should at least commit to memory the characters for 'man' (男) and 'woman' (女) on the doors.

Tourist information

The **Beijing Tourism Administration** operates a hotline for emergencies and information, tel: 12301. The English spoken at the other end is not always perfect, but if you need help or advice when you are away from your hotel, it is worth a try. Most hotels have their own travel desks for arranging rental cars and organised tours. **China International Travel Services** (CITS; tel: 6522 2991; www.cits.com.cn) is the standard national tour agency.

Make good use of the information desk or hotel concierge to check on events and opening and closing times of tourist sights. English language publications listing ongoing events are available at most major hotels, restaurants and bars.

Tours

Hundreds of tour operators eagerly seek out tourist money in a largely unregulated market so pick your tour carefully and bear in mind that many sights in and around Beijing can be reached easily by public transport. The better hotels and hostels will often provide tours to sights such as the Great Wall and Ming Tombs that offer convenience and value for money. For tailor-made tours and translation services try **Bespoke Beijing** (tel: 6528 6603; www.bespoke-beijing.com). **Beijing Xinhua International Tours** offer numerous packages to various sections of the Great Wall as well as theme tours: martial arts, cooking, bird-watching, etc (tel: 6716 0201; www.tour-beijing.com). **China Culture Centre** (tel: 6432 9341; www.chinaculture center.org) is a long-standing cultural education agency offering classes, special events and tours of Beijing.

Transport

Arrival

By air: The **Beijing Capital International Airport** (Beijing Shoudu Guoji Jichang), 30km (18 miles) from the city centre, connects the city to all parts of China and to the world's major cities.

Signage at Jianguomen subway station

For airport enquiries, call tel: 6454 1100 or visit http://en.bcia.com.cn.

You must check in at least 30 minutes before departure for a domestic flight, though an hour is probably a safer margin, and arriving two hours earlier is wise for international flights. For shorter journeys within China, the train is often a better bet. The airport tax is now included in the ticket price.

The journey between the airport and the city centre takes about 30 to 40 minutes by taxi, but allow an hour or more at busy times. Depending on the destination and category of taxi, the fare will be between 80 and 120 yuan. Beware of drivers who approach you before you reach the taxi rank; ensure the driver uses a meter, or make sure you agree on a price before setting off. The Airport Expressway has an additional 10 yuan toll fare, for which a receipt is provided. If your hotel is near the airport, drivers may be unwilling to take you unless you pay extra – this is illegal, but agreeing to pay will save you much arguing and changing of taxis. The airport express light rail links the airport to Dongzhimen subway station, which gives access to Line 2 and Line 12. The journey takes about 20 minutes, making it quicker than a taxi at rush hours. The service currently runs from Terminal 3 from 6.12am to 10.51pm and from Terminal 2 from 6.35am to 11.10pm.

By rail: Beijing has three main railway stations: Beijing Railway Station (Beijing Zhan), Beijing West (Beijing Xizhan) and Beijing South (Beijing Nanzhan). All three are accessible by subway. Some trains to other parts of China run from the city's three smaller stations. Trans-Siberian trains leave from the Beijing Railway Station for a five-day (via Mongolia) or six-day (via north-eastern China) journey to Moscow. The **Beijing International Hotel** (9 Jianguomennei Dajie; tel: 6512 0507) has an international train ticket booking office. **Monkey Business**, (tel: 6591 6519; www.monkeyshrine.com), a tour agency, specialises in trans-Siberian trips.

If you are arriving on the Trans-Siberian, the same health and customs procedures apply as for international arrivals by air. Taxis are plentiful at the Beijing Railway Station, though there is a long wait. Less expensive, although usually very crowded, are buses that will take you downtown for only 2 yuan.

For travel within China, the best place to buy tickets is the foreigners' booking office to the left of the main concourse inside the Beijing Railway Station, where you can also buy tickets for trains leaving from the Beijing West Station. Beijing West also has a foreigners' ticket office. Foreigners' ticket windows will often only sell higher-grade seats, however. If you want a sleeper berth, especially in summer or during holidays, buy your ticket at least five days in advance. Return tickets from major cit-

A subway train

ies are often available, though limited. Railways have been gradually upgraded with high-speed rail links, which dramatically reduce the time taken to get around the country.

By road: Long-distance buses connect Beijing to many cities. These include Tianjin, Chengde, Beidaihe and Taiyuan. On some routes taking the bus is faster, but generally less comfortable and less safe than taking the train. The sleeper buses operate longer routes. Beijing's main long-distance bus stations are located at Dongzhimen, Xizhimen and Yongdingmen.

By sea: The closest seaport to Beijing is neighbouring Tianjin, where ferries depart for Incheon in South Korea, and Osaka, Kobe and Shimonoseki in Japan.

Within Beijing

Taxis: Beijing is oversupplied with taxis, which are inexpensive and convenient. Prices start at 13 yuan for the first three kilometres, and rise by 2.3 yuan per kilometre thereafter. Make sure the meter is switched on before setting off, and ask for a receipt before you get out of the taxi. Drivers usually cannot speak much English. It is a good idea to have your destination and the name and address of your hotel written down in Chinese before setting off. (Hotel name cards in Chinese are very useful for this.) Drivers must post their car number and identity card inside the taxi, so you can note down these details in case of complaints. Avoid 'black cabs', unregulated private drivers that will offer to drive you for a (very inflated) fare, usually late at night or during peak hours.

Beijing's taxi drivers are generally honest. Do not assume the worst if they take convoluted routes. The city's many one-way streets and complex traffic rules forbid left turns at many junctions. But drivers who line up for hours in front of hotels are often hoping for big fares.

Taxis can also be rented for longer trips, such as whole-day tours or visits to the Great Wall or the Ming Tombs. If you plan to do this, make sure you agree to the total fare and the precise itinerary in advance. Call **Beijing Taxi** (tel: 6837 3399) or simply ask a taxi driver you have come to like.

Bus: Beijing's intricate and ever-changing bus network can be a mystery even to lifelong residents of the city. The English-language website www.bjbus.com can make things easier. Buses are slow and crowded and the distances between stops are sometimes long. On the other hand, buses are a very inexpensive means of transport. A few routes have now been improved, with air-conditioned double-decker buses plying them. Minibuses use the same routes as the buses, and although they offer a faster, more comfortable service at several times the ordinary bus fare, these prices are still low by Western

Hutong pedicab tour

standards. Bus tickets are usually 1 yuan, though they may cost more for long rides or plusher buses.

Subway: Beijing's subway system is fast, reliable and very cheap, but can be extremely crowded during rush hours and particularly at interchange stations. Currently, all journeys start at 3 yuan and increase in fare depending on distance. There are trains every few minutes from 5am until 11pm. It is easy to find your way around, especially as signs and announcements are bilingual. Buy your ticket from the ticket office window or automatic ticket machines. The machines require you to use a touch screen to select your point of departure which can be confusing. For convenience, carry coins or 10 yuan notes.

Bicycles: Many hotels have bicycles for hire; if your hotel cannot rent you one, it can advise you where to go. Budget hotels rent out bikes for around 10 yuan per day (excluding the deposit); more upmarket hotels charge in excess of 100 yuan per day or 35 yuan per hour (excluding the deposit). Shops around Houhai also rent single and two-person bikes. Be aware of bike theft, a prevalent form of crime in Beijing.

Pedicabs: If you want to experience travelling through Beijing at a cyclist's pace but don't feel up to cycling yourself, pedicabs – three-wheeled bicycles that accommodate up to two passengers at the back plus the driver in front – can be hired near many tourist sights, especially Houhai and Ritan Park, as well as at larger hotels. Some hotels have their own pedicabs at set prices. Prices are negotiable, from 5 to 30 yuan, depending on the distance you wish to travel and the time of day. Pedicabs are often more expensive than taxis, but as Beijing's rush-hour traffic jams worsen by the day, it can sometimes be faster to walk, cycle or hop into a pedicab than taking a taxi to a nearby destination.

If you are interested in taking a pedicab tour of Beijing's *hutong*, you can arrange this in advance with the **Hutong Pedicab Company** (26 Di'anmennei Xidajie; tel: 6612 3236), or simply head to the Houhai or Dazhalan areas.

Driving

Driving in Beijing is not recommended. Foreign drivers are required to go through a lengthy and costly application procedure to get a local licence (an international licence is a prerequisite). And once on the road you may regret it as traffic rules are often ignored. Companies such as **FESCO** (www.fescochina. com) and **Beijing Expats Service** (www. expatslife.com) have experience helping foreigners obtain driving licences for use in China. It is possible to rent a car and driver for several hundred yuan per day, or a few thousand a month. Try **Hertz** (tel: 800 988 1336; www.hertz.com) or **First Choice Car Rental Service** (tel: 138 1015 6525; www.fcars.cn).

Travelling by bus around Tiananmen Square

V

Visas and passports

Valid passports and visas are required of all foreign tourists. Visas may be obtained at embassies or consulates of the People's Republic of China, or through overseas offices of the state-run China International Travel Service (CITS).

Most group tourists are allowed entry through group visas. For individual travellers, single-entry visas are valid for entry within three months of issue. Visas are usually issued for 30 to 60 days, and can be extended for another 30 days in China for a small fee at the foreign affairs section of the **Public Security Bureau** (tel: 6404 7799) at Andingmen Dongdajie, just east of the Lama Temple.

Residents of 51 countries, including the UK, US, Canada and Australia, can obtain a free 72-hour visa to visit Beijing while in transit to other destinations. Note that this only applies when you are visiting one Chinese city – you cannot, for instance, enjoy a 72 hour stay in Beijing and then fly to Shanghai.

Business or study visas are issued on the presentation of a letter or a similar official document from any recognised Chinese organisation. Business travellers can be issued multi-entry visas that are valid for six months to one year.

Carry your passport with you at all times, as it will often be required when you check into hotels, make reservations and change money, as well as for bank transactions. If your passport is lost or stolen, contact your embassy and the Public Security Bureau immediately.

Be sure to leave the country before your visa expires. The fee for overstaying runs from a steep 500 yuan per day up to a maximum of 5,000 yuan.

W

Websites

The best places to find information online are probably the websites of local English-language magazines. Those for *The Beijinger* (www.thebeijinger.com), listings on *Time Out Beijing* (www.timeoutbeijing.com), City Weekend (www.cityweekend.com/beijing) and That's Beijing (www.thatsmags.com) are the most useful.

Weights and measures

China uses the metric system in almost all measurements. The only variation you are likely to encounter is food weighed and priced in jin, which is more or less half of a kilogram (called a gongjin in Chinese).

Women travellers

Women travelling alone generally experience few problems in China. Travelling by public transport or bicycle is usually safe, but there have been occasional reports of taxi drivers harassing foreign women. When taking taxis, especially at night, or visiting smaller bars and clubs, it may be better to join other tourists.

Interesting English translation

LANGUAGE

Beijingers speak Putonghua, known in the West as Mandarin Chinese. Based on the northern dialect, it is promoted as standard Chinese throughout the country, although most people also speak their local dialect. Native Beijingers, for example, also speak Beijinghua, a dialect of Putonghua. The accent in the capital is harsher than the softer southern accents, with a distinct 'er' sound added to the end of many syllables. Staff in most upscale Beijing hotels and tourist areas will be able to speak some English, but it is a good idea to write down your destination in Chinese, because taxi drivers speak little English.

Mandarin is China's official language. In addition to Mandarin, known as putong hua, most Chinese speak local dialects. Written Chinese uses characters based on pictograms, which were originally pictorial representations of ideas. Some 6,000–8,000 characters are in regular use; 3,000 are sufficient for reading a newspaper. In mainland China, simplified characters are used, while Hong Kong and Taiwan use more complex traditional characters. The standard romanisation system for Chinese characters is known as hanyu pinyin. It has been in use since 1958, and is used throughout this book.

Tones make it difficult for foreigners to speak Mandarin, as different tones give the same syllable completely different meanings. However, the pronunciation of consonants in hanyu pinyin is similar to those in English. The i after the consonants ch, c, r, sh, s, z, zh is not pronounced; it indicates that the preceding sound is lengthened.

Greetings

Hello *Nǐ hǎo* 你好
How are you? *Nǐ hǎo ma?* 你好吗?
Thank you *Xièxie* 谢谢
Goodbye *Zài jiàn* 再见
My name is... *Wǒ jiào...* 我叫...
What is your name? *Nín jiào shénme míngzì?* 您叫什么名字?
I am very happy... *Wǒ hěn gāoxìng...* 我很高兴...
Can you speak English? *Nín huì shuō Yīngyǔ ma?* 你会说英语吗?
Can you speak Chinese? *Nín huì shuō Hànyǔ ma?* 你会说汉语吗?
I cannot speak Chinese *Wǒ bù huì hànyǔ* 我不会汉语
I do not understand *Wǒ bù dǒng* 我不懂
Do you understand? *Nín dǒng ma?* 您懂吗?
Please speak a little slower *Qǐng nín shuō màn yìdiǎn* 请您说慢一点
What is this called? *Zhège jiào shénme?* 这个叫什么?
How do you say... *...Zěnme shuō?* ...怎么说?
Please *Qǐng/Xièxie* 请 / 谢谢
Sorry *Duìbuqǐ* 对不起

Recipe books at least have pictures

Travel

Where is it? *Zài nǎr?* …在哪儿?

Do you have it here? *Zhèr… yǒu ma?* 这儿有…吗?

No/it's not here/there aren't any *Méi yǒu* 没有

Hotel *Fàndiàn/bīnguǎn* 饭店/宾馆

Restaurant *Fànguǎn* 饭馆

Bank *Yínháng* 银行

Post office *Yóujú* 邮局

Toilet *Cèsuǒ* 厕所

Railway station *Huǒchē zhàn* 火车站

Bus station *Qìchē zhàn* 汽车站

Embassy *Dàshǐguǎn* 大使馆

Consulate *Lǐngshìguǎn* 领事馆

Passport *Hùzhào* 护照

Visa *Qiānzhèng* 签证

Pharmacy *Yàodiàn* 药店

Hospital *Yīyuàn* 医院

Doctor *Dàifu/yīshēng* 大夫/医生

Translate *Fānyì* 翻译

Do you have…? *Nín yǒu… ma* 您有…吗?

I want to go to… *Wǒ yào qù…* 我要去…

I want/I would like *Wǒ yào/wǒ xiǎng yào* 我要/我想要

I want to buy… *Wǒ xiǎng mǎi…* 我想买…

Shopping

How much does it cost? *Zhège duōshǎo qián?* 这个多少钱?

Too expensive, thank you *Tài guì le, xièxie* 太贵了，谢谢

Money, hotels, transport, communications

Money *Qián* 钱

Credit card *Xìnyòngkǎ* 信用卡

Foreign currency *Wàihuìquàn* 外汇钱

Where can I change money? *Zài nǎr kěyǐ huàn qián?* 在哪儿可以还钱?

What is the exchange rate? *Bǐjià shì duōshǎo?* 比价是多少?

We want to stay for one (two/three) nights *Wǒmen xiǎng zhù yì (liǎng/sān) tiān* 我们想住一(两，三)天

How much is the room per day? *Fángjiān duōshǎo qián yì tiān?* 房间多少钱一天?

Room number *Fángjiān hàomǎ* 房间号码

Reception *Qiántái/fúwùtái* 前台 / 服务台

Key *Yàoshi* 钥匙

Luggage *Xíngli* 行李

Airport *Fēijīchǎng* 飞机场

Bus *Gōnggòng qìchē* 公共汽车

Taxi *Chūzū qìchē* 出租汽车

Bicycle *Zìxíngchē* 自行车

Telephone *Diànhuà* 电话

Use the Internet *Shàngwǎng* 上网

Eating out

Waiter/waitress *Fúwùyuán/xiǎojiě* 服务员/小姐

Menu *Càidān* 菜单

Chopsticks *Kuàizi* 筷子

Knife *Dāozi* 刀子

Fork *Chāzi* 叉子

Spoon *Sháozi* 勺子

I am a vegetarian *Wǒ shì chī sù de rén* 我是吃素的人

Beer *Píjiǔ* 啤酒

Red/white wine *Hóng/bái pú táo jiǔ* 红/白葡萄酒

Green/black tea *Lǜchá/hóngchá* 绿茶 / 红茶

Coffee *Kāfēi* 咖啡

Ducks on Houhai Lake

Beef/pork/lamb/chicken *Niúròu/zhūròu/yángròu/jīròu* 牛肉/猪肉/羊肉/鸡肉

Spicy/sweet/sour/salty *Là/tián/suān/xián* 辣/甜/酸/咸

Can we have the bill, please *Qǐng jié zhàng/mǎidān* 请结账 / 买单

Numbers

One/two/three/four/five *Yī/ér/sān/sì/wǔ* 一/二/三/四/五

Six/seven/eight/nine/ten *Liù/qī/bā/jiǔ/shí* 六/七/八/九/十

Eleven/twelve/twenty/thirty/forty *Shíyī/shíèr/èrshí/sānshí/sìshí* 十一/十二/二十/三十/四十

Fifty/sixty/seventy/eighty/ninety *Wǔshí/liùshí/qīshí/bāshí/jiǔshí* 五十/六十/七十/八十/九十

One hundred *Yībǎi* 一百

One thousand *Yìqiān* 一千

Place names in Chinese

English *Hanyu Pinyin* Chinese

798 Art District *798 Yishùqū* 798艺术区

Ancient Observatory *Gǔguān Xiàngtái* 古观象台

Beihai Park *Běihǎi Gōngyuán* 北海公园

Beijing Botanical Gardens *Běijīng Zhíwùyuán* 北京植物园

Bell Tower *Zhōnglóu* 钟楼

Blue Zoo *Fùguó Hǎidǐ Shìjiè* 富国海底世界

Caochangdi *Cǎochǎngdì* 草场地

Changling *Chánglíng* 长陵

Chengde *Chéng Dé* 承德

Chi'enmen 23 *Qiánmén èrshísān hào* 前门23号

China World Trade Centre *Zhōngguó Guójì Màoyì Zhōngxīn* 中国国际贸易中心

Chinese Ethnic Culture Park *Zhōngguó Mínzúyuán* 中国民族园

Coal Hill (Jingshan) Park *Jǐngshān Gōngyuán* 景山公园

Confucius Temple *Kǒng Miào* 孔庙

Cuandixia *Cuāndǐxià* 爨底下

Daguanlou Cinema *Dàguānlóu* 大观楼

Dashanzi *Dàshānzi* 大山子

Dazhalan Street *Dàzhálán Jiē* 大栅栏街

Dingling *Dìnglíng* 定陵

Ditan Park *Dìtán Gōngyuán* 地坛公园

Donghuamen Night Market *Dōnghuámén Yèshìchǎng* 东华门夜市场

Dongsi Shitiao *Dōngsì Shítiáo* 东四十条

Double-Stone Village *Shuāngshítóu* 双石头

Drum Tower *Gǔlóu* 鼓楼

Forbidden City *Gùgōng/Zǐjìnchéng* 故宫/紫禁城

Foreign Legation Quarter *Dōngjiāomín Xiàng* 东交民巷

Fragrant Hills Park *Xiāngshān Gōngyuán* 香山公园

FunDazzle *Fāndǒulè* 翻斗乐

Great Hall of the People *Rénmín Dàhuìtáng* 人民大会堂

Great Wall *Wànlǐ Cháng Chéng* 万里长城

Guanghua Buddhist Temple *Guānghuà Sì* 广化寺

Hongqiao Market *Hóngqiáo Shìchǎng* 红桥市场

Houhai (Rear Lake) *Hòu Hǎi* 后海

Huanghuacheng *Huánghuāchéng* 黄花城

Imperial Academy *Guózǐjiàn* 国子监

Imperial City Art Gallery *Huángchéng*

Practising calligraphy in Beihai Park

BOOKS AND FILM

Film

China's film industry has come a long way since 1913 when its first home-grown movie, Nanfu Nanqi, a 45-minute short about forced marriages, was released. Zhang Yimou's **Hero** was a box-office hit in the US in 2002, and Chinese directors and actors are slowly gaining international recognition, a few even flirting with Hollywood – actresses Gong Li and Zhang Ziyi both starred in the 2005 romantic drama **Memoirs of a Geisha**. Art-house directors are frequently fêted at film festivals, and Beijing is one of the best places to pick up subtitled DVDs of their works.

Pre-1949, the Chinese movie industry, largely based in Shanghai, was heavily influenced by American cinema, and comedies and martial arts flicks were standard. After the Communist revolution, movies were considered great propaganda tools, filmmakers were sent to study in Russia, and the centre of the country's movie industry shifted from Shanghai to Beijing with the establishment of the prestigious Beijing Film Academy. In the mid-1980s, along with the opening and reform period, the so-called 'fifth generation' of film directors brought Chinese film to the attention of the international festival circuit. Two of these, Zhang Yimou (**Red Sorghum**, **Raise the Red Lantern**, **Hero**, **Not One Less**), and Chen Kaige (**Yellow Earth**, **Farewell My Concubine**) are China's most famous directors today. Their work was celebrated for its range of style and its break from the socialist realism of the Mao era. After the Tiananmen crackdown of 1989, several directors moved overseas.

By the mid-nineties, a new breed of directors, called the 'sixth generation', had emerged. Their work is distinct from their predecessors' as being edgier, grittier and more budget in production, almost documentary-like. Some names from this movement include Wang Xiaoshuai (**Be jing Bicycle**), Jia Zhangke (**Platform**, **The World**) and Li Yang (**Blind Shaft**). Their movies are raw, exposing the uglier side of modern 'capitalist' China.

The work of these independent filmmakers goes largely unnoticed at home; it is the slapsticks, thrillers and romantic comedies such as **Green Hat**, **Crazy Stone** and **If You Are the One** that do well. Big period epics such as Peter Chan's **The Warlords** (2007), Zhang Yimou's **Curse of the Golden Flower** (2006) and Chen Kaige's **The Promise** (2005) are liked by both the government and foreign film fans but are not so hot with the Chinese public. While the government limits the flow of foreign blockbusters that can be screened here to a trickle, they still prove to be reliable hits and are increasingly important to Hollywood studio budgets: films like 2014's **Transformers: The Age of Extinction** made more than $300 million.

'Raise the Red Lantern'

Literature

The written word is so revered in China that calligraphy has developed into an art unto itself. Literary scholars have always garnered respect; Mao himself was a poet. Classical texts take some work to plough through, but contemporary authors shed a fascinating insight on modern culture and are also increasingly being translated into English. Beijing has a vibrant book culture with several giant bookstores, many of which also offer a good selection of foreign-language titles, albeit under the restrictions of government censorship.

The earliest examples of Chinese literature emerged around 5,000 years ago. Writings were largely confined to philosophical and religious texts such as the *I Ching* (Book of Changes), a Daoist treatise on predicting the future. Chinese poetry reached its zenith during the Tang dynasty which nurtured such poetic greats as Li Bai, Du Fu and Wang Wei.

It wasn't until the Ming dynasty, that the Chinese novel emerged. Scholars have come up with a definitive quartet of the best and most influential books from this period: namely *Romance of the Three Kingdoms*, *Outlaws of the Marsh*, *Journey to the West* and *Dream of the Red Chamber*. They have had a tremendous impact on Chinese and Asian cultures and their stories appear in a host of TV dramas, films and computer games.

After the fall of the last dynasty, novelists largely abandoned the historical and romantic epic and instead started writing in the vernacular and exploring political and nationalistic themes. The most famous of these was Lu Xun, oft called the 'father of modern Chinese literature.' He was an ardent leftist and thus his stories became favourite set texts in schools in China post-1949. Under Mao, the only literature that was allowed was Socialist Realism that aimed to promote the idea of a Communist state.

The modern Chinese novel covers ground as broad as any in the West, although if you want your book published in the People's Republic you cannot criticise the government or delve too much into sex, drugs or crime. The Cultural Revolution is now fair game. Famous banned titles include 'bad girl' prose, such as Mian Mian's *Candy* and Wei Hui's *Shanghai Baby*, and the 'hooligan' novels of Wang Shuo, which frequently explore the underbelly of Beijing's darker society.

Some of the most influential contemporary authors to look out for are Su Tong (*Raise the Red Lantern*, *Rice*) whose historical fiction delves into the darker, brutal sides of human nature; Yu Hua (*To Live*) whose novel *Brothers*, a black comedy, was a best seller; and satirist Mo Yan (*Red Sorghum*, *The Republic of Wine*), whom *Time* magazine calls the 'most widely pirated of all Chinese writers.' Mo, whose pen name translates to 'no speech', won mainland China's first Nobel Prize for Literature for his magical realist literature in 2012. Also look out for Jiang Rong's *Wolf Totem*, which won the inaugural Man Asian Booker prize in 2007.

ABOUT THIS BOOK

This *Explore Guide* has been produced by the editors of Insight Guides, whose books have set the standard for visual travel guides since 1970. With top-quality photography and authoritative recommendations, these guidebooks bring you the very best routes and itineraries in the world's most exciting destinations.

BEST ROUTES

The routes in the book provide something to suit all budgets, tastes and trip lengths. As well as covering the destination's many classic attractions, the itineraries track lesser-known sights, and there are also excursions for those who want to extend their visit outside the city. The routes embrace a range of interests, so whether you are an art fan, a gourmet, a history buff or have kids to entertain, you will find an option to suit.

We recommend reading the whole of a route before setting out. This should help you to familiarise yourself with it and enable you to plan where to stop for refreshments – options are shown in the 'Food and Drink' box at the end of each tour.

For our pick of the tours by theme, consult Recommended Routes for… (see pages 6–7).

INTRODUCTION

The routes are set in context by this introductory section, giving an overview of the destination to set the scene, plus background information on food and drink, shopping and more, while a succinct history timeline highlights the key events over the centuries.

DIRECTORY

Also supporting the routes is a Directory chapter, with a clearly organised A–Z

of practical information, our pick of where to stay while you are there and select restaurant listings; these eateries complement the more low-key cafés and restaurants that feature within the routes and are intended to offer a wider choice for evening dining. Also included here are some nightlife listings, plus a handy language guide and our recommendations for books and films about the destination.

ABOUT THE AUTHORS

Sean Silbert is a freelance writer, magazine editor and all around advocate of fun times in Beijing. He gluttonously ate his way through the city as the food and drinks editor for *Time Out Beijing*, and later delved deeper into the city's growth and culture writing for publications like the *Los Angeles Times* and CNN. When not tapping away at his keyboard, he can usually be found cycling his way through the hutongs. Perhaps it's a sign of a long-term expat, but he believes one of the best ways to get in touch with Chinese culture is through food. Even so, he still is in continual search of that perfect dumpling place.

This book builds on original content by Eric Abrahamsen.

CONTACT THE EDITORS

We hope you find this Explore Guide useful, interesting and a pleasure to read. If you have any questions or feedback on the text, pictures or maps, please do let us know. If you have noticed any errors or outdated facts, or have suggestions for places to include on the routes, we would be delighted to hear from you. Please drop us an email at hello@insightguides.com. Thanks!

CREDITS

Explore Beijing
Editor: Sarah Clark
Author: Sean Silbert
Head of Production: Rebeka Davies
Picture Editor: Tom Smyth
Cartography: original cartography
Berndtson & Berndtson, updated by Carte
Photo credits: Alamy 136; Corbis 22, 23;
Getty Images 1, 10/11, 89, 91L; Hilton
Hotles & Resorts 96; Hin Mun Lee/Apa
Publications 4MC, 4/5T, 6TL, 6BC, 7MR,
7M, 8/9T, 10, 12/13, 59, 71, 84T, 85L,
84/85, 92MR, 108, 109L, 108/109, 110,
110/111, 120/121; iStock 66/67, 88,
90; Kempinski Hotels 99; Kobal 137; Leon-
ardo 92/93T, 98; Ming Tang-Evans/Apa
Publications 4ML, 4MR, 4MR, 6MC, 6ML,
6/7T, 7MR, 8ML, 8MC, 8ML, 8MC, 8MR,
8MR, 14, 14/15, 17L, 16/17, 18, 20/21,
24ML, 24MC, 24MR, 24ML, 24MC, 24MR,
24/25T, 26, 27L, 26/27, 28, 29L, 28/29,
31L, 30/31, 32, 32/33, 34, 35L, 34/35,
36, 37L, 36/37, 38, 39L, 38/39, 40, 41L,
40/41, 42, 43L, 42/43, 44, 45L, 44/45,
46, 47L, 46/47, 48, 49L, 48/49, 50, 51L,
52, 52/53, 54, 54/55, 56, 57L, 56/57, 58,
60, 61L, 60/61, 62, 62/63, 64, 64/65, 68,
68/69, 70, 72, 72/73, 74, 75L, 74/75,
76, 76/77, 78, 79L, 78/79, 84B, 86, 87L,
86/87, 92MC, 92ML, 94/95, 96/97, 102,
103L, 102/103, 104, 106/107, 112, 113,
114/115, 116, 122/123, 124/125, 126,
130, 132, 133, 134, 134/135; Nowitz
Photography/Apa Publications 4MC, 4ML,
16, 18/19, 20, 30, 50/51, 80, 81L, 80/81,
82, 82/83, 92ML, 92MC, 104/105, 106,
116/117, 118, 118/119, 122, 124,
126/127, 128, 128/129, 130/131; Peter
Stuckings/Apa Publications 120; Shangri-
La Hotels & Resorts 92MR, 100, 101;
Shutterstock 90/91
Cover credits: Shutterstock (main & BL)

Printed by Markono Print Media Pte Ltd

All Rights Reserved
© 2016 Apa Digital (CH) AG and
Apa Publications (UK) Ltd

First Edition 2016

DISTRIBUTION

Worldwide
APA Publications (Singapore) Pte
7030 Ang Mo Kio Ave 5, 08-65
Northstar @ AMK, Singapore 569880
Email: apasin@singnet.com.sg
UK and Ireland
Dorling Kindersley Ltd
(a Penguin Company)
80 Strand, London, WC2R 0RL, UK
Email: sales@uk.dk.com
US
Ingram Publisher Services
One Ingram Blvd, PO Box 3006, La Vergne,
TN 37086-1986
Email: ips@ingramcontent.com
Australia and New Zealand
Woodslane
10 Apollo St, Warriewood NSW 2102,
Australia
Email: info@woodslane.com.au

INDEX

MAP LEGEND

●	Start of tour	✉	Main post office
→	Tour & route direction	⚤	Statue/monument
❶	Recommended sight	⚱	Tower
❷	Recommended restaurant/café	ᴍ̂	Museum/gallery
★	Place of interest	⚘	Theatre
❶	Tourist information	✛	Hospital
✈	International airport	✛	Cathedral/church
🚌	Main bus station	⌂	Temple
Ⓖ	Metro Station	⚑	Beach
═	Railway	⚑	Lighthouse
•—	Cable car/Funicular rail	☀	Viewpoint
---	Ferry route	⚭	Cave
═══	Freeway	▲	Summit
⊖	Border control	∴	Ancient Site

National boundary — · —
Regional boundary - · - -
Important building
Hotel
Transport hub
Shopping /market
Pedestrian area
Urban area
Non-urban area
Park
National park
Marsh

Steps
Tunnel

INSIGHTGUIDES.COM

The Insight Guides website offers a unique way to plan and book tailor-made trips online. Be inspired by our curated destination content, read our daily travel blog and build your own dream trip from our range of customisable experiences, created by our local experts.

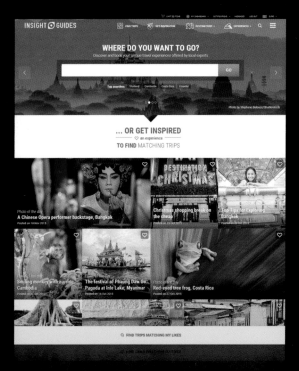

Visit our homepage and be inspired by our selection of fascinating travel stories, stunning photography and lively blogs.

Choose your dream trip from our carefully selected range of destinations, devised by trusted local experts.

Customise your perfect trip – choose your hotel, add experiences and excursions – and book securely online.

INSIGHT  GUIDES

TRAVEL MADE EASY. ASK LOCAL EXPERTS.